Instruction
MANUAL
for the 21st Century Samurai

BY
Alexei Maxim
RUSSELL

Instruction Manual for the 21st Century Samurai

Instruction Manual for the 21st Century Samurai

Copyright © 2013 Alexei Maxim Russell
All rights reserved.
ISBN: 1481961861
ISBN-13: 978-1481961868

COVER ART AND ILLUSTRATIONS PROVIDED FOR EXCLUSIVE USE IN
THIS PUBLICATION BY IRENESKA DESIGN OF MANITOBA, CANADA.

Instruction Manual for the 21st Century Samurai

TABLE OF CONTENTS

Section	Chapter	Page
1.1	Prologue	4
1.2	The Three Masters	6
1.3.1	The Ten Areas of Life	12
1.3.1.1	Career	13
1.3.1.2	Dreams	18
1.3.1.3	Love	26
1.3.1.4	Children	32
1.3.1.5	Death	38
1.3.1.6	Spiritual	42
1.3.1.7	Conflict	49
1.3.1.8	Family	61
1.3.1.9	Arts and Education	67
1.3.1.10	Leisure	73
1.4	Reference	79
1.5	Quick Reference	82
1.6	Bibliography	84

Instruction Manual for the 21st Century Samurai

1.1 Prologue

1.1.1 Purpose of this book

Who hasn't considered, at some point in their life, what it would take to live as a samurai? Whether it was a serous, life-long obsession or a passing, whimsical thought; in either case, there was really no way to know how to go about living life as a samurai. Unlike the medieval knights of Europe or the fabled amazons of ancient Greece, the warrior class of the Japanese samurai died out only a few short generations ago. And yet, to know how they behaved, by what code they lived and how they saw the world would require either a PhD in Japanese antiquities or a journey to Japan, in search of those few people who still hand down the traditions.

Any book about the samurai, or their codes, was either so strictly historical or so thickly academic that it didn't give any practical solutions to the average person, about how to go about applying the samurai ethic to their daily life. The common person, wishing to learn how to live as one of this warrior class had no resource at all. That is, until this book was written. Previously, the aspiring samurai had no resource. But now, they have the manual. Based on the ancient and authoritative texts of three samurai masters, this manual gives the direct and authentic "samurai solution" to any of life's many situations.

This pocket-sized book can be carried anywhere, anytime, for quick reference.

No matter where life takes you, you are just one quick reference away from the "samurai solution" to your problems. Men, women and children, from all walks of life; no matter who you are or what circumstances life throws your way--with this manual, you, too, can live like a samurai!

1.1.2 The history of this book

The idea for this manual was something that grew over a lifetime. I fall into the "life-long obsession" category, as far as contemplating the samurai life goes. From my first exposure to the notion of the fabled warriors, as a child, the idea colored my life. My life would inevitably take on a "Japanesque" flavor; my interior decoration would always end up looking something like a Samurai's tent; and my journeys through life would irresistibly come to resemble the very "Zen" spartanism of the wandering ronin(masterless samurai) of legend. Even my work, as a fiction writer, would inevitably take on an adventure element--in the best tradition of the great and fearless work of the dedicated samurai warrior. Given this obsession and an equally strong obsession with logic and order, it may have been inevitable that a "samurai manual" was somewhere on this ronin's path.

In search of such a thing, I had systematically read all major modern works about the samurai. While informative and scholarly, I was always left frustrated at the lack of ready and accessible practical advice for the aspiring modern-day samurai. I had read the works of the ancient masters as well, but their teachings were so broad and so often put in metaphor and old-fashioned language, that it was difficult to glean the ancient wisdom from them and put them into a simple form that I could apply to my life.

And so, being unable to find such a "manual" to samurai living, I decided to create one. I distilled the basic messages from the works of three legendary samurai masters--choosing only the most essential and basic elements of their messages--and cross-referenced it with any situation that a modern person may find themselves in. With a book that fits in your pocket, and a quick reference index for finding speedy solutions, there is no longer any obstacle for those of you who, like me, are aspiring modern-day samurai.

Instruction Manual for the 21st Century Samurai

1.2 The Three Masters

1.2.1 Musashi Miyamoto (Book of Five Rings) 1584 - 1645 The Ronin

1.2.1.1 History
Considered one of the greatest warriors of all time, Miyamoto was a samurai of legendary prowess. But most of his life was spent on the road, as a wandering ronin. The world was his teacher and his journeys have been left to us in legend. These legends tell of his flawless record of winning duels, even from a very early age. His winning tactics eventually led to the founding of the famous Niten-ryu style of swordsmanship. Not only a strong-arm, Miyamoto had profound insights into life and a complex and original spiritual outlook.

All these philosophies, as well as his fighting strategies, are outlined in his famous work "The Book of Five Rings", which is still studied today as one of the all-time classics of strategy and warrior philosophy.

1.2.1.2 Philosophy
The title of "The Book of Five Rings" most likely refers to the fact that the book is divided into five sections, which correspond with the five Japanese elements: Earth, Water, Fire, Wind and the Void (also interpreted as "heaven"). The first section, called the "ground book", lays the groundwork for Miyamoto's life philosophy. This is the most important of the sections, as it explains the fundamentals of what makes a warrior, not only in fencing, but in all things. It also contains Miyamoto's own personal warrior's code, which we will call the "strategy code." This code can be summed up into the following nine points:
1. Do not think dishonestly.
2. The Way is in the training.
3. Become acquainted with every art.
4. Know the Ways of all professions.
5. Distinguish between gain and loss in worldly matters.

Instruction Manual for the 21st Century Samurai

1.2.1 Musashi Miyamoto (Book of Five Rings)

6. Develop intuitive judgment and understanding for everything.
7. Perceive those things which cannot be seen.
8. Pay attention even to trifles.
9. Do nothing which is of no use.

Some of these points may seem vague, but Miyamoto was trying to distill, into a very few words, all the wisdom he had gained, as a warrior. There is actually a deeper meaning in every one of these nine points. This section is only an introduction to Miyamoto's philosophy; we will explore these nine points in a practical sense in the later sections of this book, as they apply to various life situations.

Some of Miyamoto's philosophies contrast sharply with that of the established palace samurai. For example, Miyamoto considered it essential for a warrior to "distinguish between gain and loss in worldly matters" whereas Yamamoto stated that "calculating people are contemptible. The reason for this is that calculation deals with loss and gain." It is likely that living "on the streets" and not in luxurious palaces made ronin like Miyamoto more "practical" about matters like loss and gain. Conflicting ideals like this demonstrate the difference between the samurai elite and the humble ronin.

But, to get a well-rounded view of the samurai warrior, and to emulate them with full authenticity, it is advisable to take the best points from both classes of samurai warrior. After all, there is more in common than in contrast, between the two. They likely followed the same general code of the samurai, called "Bushido code" in addition to their own personal code of ethics. Another similarity is illustrated by Miyamoto's definition of a samurai as one who has "acceptance of death". This is a basic samurai definition which is shared by Miyamoto, Yamamoto and by the Zen Buddhist monk, Dogen. Buddhism, after all, preaches accepting death and change.

Instruction Manual for the 21st Century Samurai

1.2.2 Yamamoto Tsunetomo (Hagakure) 1659 - 1719 The General

1.2.2.1 History

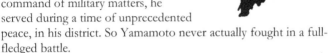

Yamamoto was a noble samurai who served his lord loyally for over 30 years. Although he had a full command of military matters, he served during a time of unprecedented peace, in his district. So Yamamoto never actually fought in a full-fledged battle.

Yamamoto may not have fought countless duels, like that wandering ronin of the roads, Miyamoto, but he came from a long line of highly experienced battle commanders. On top of that, he knew all the social graces and could give us a personal view into the life and outlooks of the traditional samurai of the lord's castle. The result is a snapshot of the many sacred codes of the samurai, collectively known as "bushido." After his master's death, he retired to a mountain retreat and became a stoic hermit. Dictating to a fellow samurai, he shared a life-time of experience, living life as a traditional samurai, and left a book called "Hagakure". This book preserved, for all time, many of the codes and traditions that made up the "bushido" of the established samurai.

1.2.2.2 Philosophy

The Hagakure is actually a series of conversations with Yamamoto, after he was already quite old. He talks about what was expected of a palace samurai, right down to matters of personal hygiene. Like Miyamoto, he was led by a stringent warrior code. His code was called the "Nibeshima code." This was the code of the Nabeshima clan, which Yamamoto served. It consisted of the following four points:
1. Never to be outdone in the Way of the Samurai (Bushido code).
2. To be of good use to the master.
3. To be filial to my parents.

1.2.2 Yamamoto Tsunetomo (Hagakure)

4. To manifest great compassion, and to act for the sake of Man (meaning humankind).

Yamamoto was more conservative than Miyamoto, in many ways, and it is reflected in his slightly different personal code. For example, Miyamoto considered it important to be "acquainted with all arts" and "know the Ways of all professions" whereas Yamamoto considered it inappropriate for a samurai to be anything but a warrior, although he did accept the practice of art in certain cases. For example, the practice of calligraphy--with its spartan simplicity--was considered very "Zen." Being a "gentleman warrior" type of art, it was acceptable to practice it--so long as there were no battles to be fought. But, in spite of their differences, it is likely both Miyamoto and Yamamoto both followed the prevailing "bushido code" of the day. Although not invented by the three masters, Yamamoto makes reference to it in his vows; Miyamoto, no doubt, followed them, in addition to his personal nine point "strategy code". No samurai manual is complete without mention of this "bushido code." The seven point code is as follows:

1. Rectitude. Be an example of decency.
2. Courage. Be an example of fearlessness.
3. Benevolence. Be an example of compassion.
4. Respect. Be an example of politeness.
5. Honesty. Be an example of truth.
6. Honor. Be an example of good reputation.
7. Loyalty. Be an example of trustworthiness.

Taken together, this may seem like a lot to remember and a lot of codes. But don't worry! You don't need to remember all this right now. The usefulness of this book is that, when met with a situation, you can use the quick reference section and find the part of the samurai codes that best applies to your situation. You will be given the right reference and so you will instantly know what to do. You will always be only one quick reference away from the authentic and most appropriate "samurai solution."

Instruction Manual for the 21st Century Samurai

1.2.3 Eihei Dōgen
(Shōbōgenzō)
1200 - 1253 The Monk

1.2.3.1 History

Dōgen was not exactly a samurai master, in the strict sense. He never carried a sword or fought a battle. All his battles were spiritual. He was the most famous monk of a school of Buddhism called "Zen". The preferred religion of the samurai, the ideas of Zen Buddhism account for a lot of the samurai's warrior code and how they looked at life. Dōgen is credited with founding the first school of Zen Buddhism in Japan. The Zen school was previously only available in China and was called "Chen".

Because Dōgen brought the samurai religion to the samurai of Japan, and was one of its most esteemed monks, we can consider him more than worthy of the position as one of our three samurai masters, with or without a sword. His most major work, "Shōbōgenzō", outlines the main tenets of Zen Buddhism and is widely considered to be an authoritative work on the subject.

1.2.3.2 Philosophy

The term "Shōbōgenzō" actually refers to the oral tradition left behind by the Buddha himself and passed on for generations by the enlightened masters. These traditions were passed to Dōgen during a visit to China. On his return to Japan, he wrote these traditions out in the form of "Shōbōgenzō".

The words of the master are deep and meaningful. Monks spend years or decades in Zen monasteries trying to fully penetrate the gems of enlightenment left behind by Dōgen. But it can basically be summed up in the fact that Dōgen rejected the idea that reciting sutras and praying to the Buddha was the best path to

1.2.3 Eihei Dōgen (Shōbōgenzō)

enlightenment--as preached by other Buddhists. Dōgen brought, to Japan, a form of meditation called zazen. Zazen was an active form of meditation, which was constant and encompassed all daily activities.

Instead of sitting and meditating for hours, then returning to "normal" consciousness, the zazen practitioner taught themselves to meditate at all moments: when sitting, when walking, when eating, when sweeping the floor. Dōgen believed any less than this did not bring enlightenment easily and did not teach the student the full significance of enlightenment. He believed that unless you "live" enlightenment, you will never be fully enlightened. This is the heart of Zen and Dōgen's teachings.

Because Zen Buddhism preaches the usual Buddhist ideals of accepting death and change and abandoning personal desire, it was the ideal spiritual partner to the samurai, who could die at any moment and who was expected to take bravery, loyalty and self-sacrifice to almost super-human levels. Zazen allowed the samurai to race into the fray with a light heart, as they had no fear of leaving a physical world towards which they were not particularly attached. This is the Zen way of living.

We too, can benefit from zazen. The exact meaning of "enlightenment" is hard to explain and even harder to understand, and we will not go so far as to try to become enlightened Buddhas. But we can go so far as to take some of the gems of wisdom from Shōbōgenzō and apply them to our life situations, to help us learn to respond to life in a more "Zen" way – as befitting the aspiring 21st century samurai. This will be enough for the purposes of this manual.

1.3.1 The Ten Areas of Life

This manual divides life into ten sections: 1. Career, 2. Dreams, 3. Love, 4. Children, 5. Death, 6. Spirituality, 7. Conflict, 8. Family, 9. Arts and Education, 10. Leisure.

Within these ten sections, we cover all the major areas of life, and can apply the appropriate "samurai solution" to any situation life throws at us! If you find yourself in a fix and ask yourself, "what would the three samurai masters do?", merely open up this book in the chapter titled "reference", identify the problem most closely resembling your own and you will pointed to the appropriate "samurai solution" to solve your problem like a samurai! If you cannot find a problem near enough to your own, or if you are really in a hurry, you can access "quick reference" section, look for the word which best describes your problem and proceed from there!

This manual seeks to preserve and encourage the ethical excellence and extraordinary warrior ways of the samurai by making it easily accessible and understandable to the modern aspiring samurai. Not only will this manual serve as the pocket-book for the new generation of samurai warrior, but you are encouraged to join our community of 21st century samurai, at the following social media website: www.samuraicollective.com. Together, we can offer encouragement, share our successes, discuss the finer points of the samurai life and even form real-world connections to establish local samurai groups, within our respective communities.

Anything is possible when true samurai get together. But, at the very least, if this manual can succeed in giving direction to all those who have aspired to the warrior life and longed for the authentic life of the samurai, then it would have fulfilled its purpose entirely.

We can then claim a victory for the historical samurai, worthy of legend's most honored and accomplished shogunate.

Instruction Manual for the 21st Century Samurai

1.3.1.1 Career

A samurai approaches his or her career, primarily, as a battlefield. This doesn't mean your workplace should be full of blood and conflict. In fact, the three masters do not recommend aggression; conflict should be a last resort. For dealing with conflict and aggression, it is more appropriate to read the chapter titled "Conflict"(1.3.1.7). By saying that our career should be a battlefield doesn't mean violence; it means the same samurai outlook that helped them deal with battles will also help us to carry out our career plans. We will use the same perspective and strategies as the samurai did, to help achieve our career dreams.

A workplace requires training and the development of mastery. Miyamoto stated that "The Way is in the training". Similarly, Yamamoto said, "advance daily, becoming more skillful than today... This is never-ending" and that a samurai "remains consistently undistracted twenty-four hours a day." These things show the general firmness of the samurai work ethic. In general, this is how the samurai honed their preparedness for battle. Like a battlefield, our career requires bravery, leadership, action, planning, training, strategy and ambition to advance ever further. In all these ways, our career is like a battlefield and the masters have insights into battle preparedness.

Yamamoto is the best source of information about this. Due to the fact that, of the three masters, Yamamoto was the only one with lengthy experience handling "employees", "bosses" and a full-fledged career, as a martial retainer. But Miyamoto had some insights into battlefield readiness, which could aid in our career strategy. The wisdom of the masters can be divided into three areas. These areas are 1. Leadership, 2. Learning and Mistakes, 3. Colleagues. By studying the "samurai solution" for these three areas, we can learn to approach our career with the confidence and efficiency of a samurai.

Instruction Manual for the 21st Century Samurai

1.3.1.1.1 Leadership

"The way of the Samurai is one of immediacy."

Whether you're an executive, a supervisor or a tradesperson on a project, you will need to make decisions. Even the humblest of jobs requires independent decision-making. Whether you are the boss or the one who sweeps the streets--making solid, practical decisions is a part of every job and is the essence of leadership. The reason why I do not call this area "decisions" is because, when you think of it, leadership is the ability to make clear, quick decisions and to carry them through with confidence. And so, "decisions" and "leadership" are the same thing. Anyone who is good at their job makes decisions like a leader, whether they are actually "the boss" or not. In this way, we are all leaders, in our particular careers. So, how do we make decisions and lead our career like a samurai commander?

Yamamoto believed that a samurai should, above all, be decisive. This didn't mean that you should act impulsively, without forethought. It meant that a samurai should develop quick judgment and, once you have decided on something, you should follow your plans through with decisive confidence. Yamamoto recommended that you learn to make decisions within "seven breaths." So, how can you learn to do that, without making rash, poorly-thought-out decisions?

Yamamoto recommended a samurai always study, tirelessly, and "without putting things off ." That way, you will be well prepared for any decision you need to make, at work, because you've studied your workplace thoroughly beforehand. This allows you to make quick, decisive choices, and still be able to make wise, practical decisions.

The ronin, Miyamoto, had a similar idea in mind when he advised aspiring sword fighters to "develop intuitive judgment". What he

Instruction Manual for the 21st Century Samurai

1.3.1.1 Career

meant here, was to learn to make very accurate but very quick choices. It helped Miyamoto to win duels; it helped Yamomoto's revered ancestors to win battles; and it can help us to win at work.

So, what is the samurai solution to the question of leadership in our career? Decisiveness. Study your career tirelessly, during your free time. Know your job inside out. And when you are at work, use that knowledge to make quick, sharp decisions; forceful, confident choices that will make you a powerful force in your career. Whether it means you clean the streets better than anyone on earth and are recognized as a cut above all the rest; or whether it means you lead your company through a thousand successful battles, as its decisive leader, you will have successfully learned how to lead and make decisions like a samurai.

1.3.1.1.2 Learning and making mistakes

"A man who has never once erred is dangerous."

Yamamoto believed that you should always learn; you should always look at what you know and be able to say "This is not enough". And so, it was a definite fact that a samurai was very friendly with mistakes. In our modern world, we look unkindly on mistakes and imperfection, but this is far from the samurai ideal. Mistakes are part of the learning process and if you haven't made them then you are, indeed, dangerous because it means you have never learned anything. Mistakes, to a samurai, are the proof of your learning. In fact, Yamamoto stated that he would not trust a samurai under his command unless they had lost their job at least seven times, under previous lords. Because, as he put it, "seven times down, eight times up." Anyone with the power to endure and learn from seven big mistakes and still crawl back up to an honored position in life is a samurai of phenomenal learning and endurance.

Instruction Manual for the 21st Century Samurai

1.3.1.1 Career

Yamamoto not only extolled the virtues of failure, but he suggested that a samurai should instantly admit any mistake, without a moment's hesitation. This clashes with our stereotypical image of the over-proud warrior who is too macho to admit he made a mistake. To a samurai, such blind egotism is a sign of weakness and a mind that doesn't understand Zen Buddhist ideas, which are generally against egotism. A samurai understands Zen Buddhism; a samurai also thinks like a commander--coolly minimizing damage with a detached and intelligent mind. As Yamamoto put it, "if one will rectify his mistakes, their traces will soon disappear." It would be a great disgrace for a samurai to prolong the negative effect of a mistake and incur such unnecessary damage because of blind, stubborn egotism.

So, what is the samurai solution to learning on the job? Always learn and never be afraid to learn from your mistakes. The samurai approach to learning was very much connected to the attitude they took towards failure. In typical samurai fashion, they focused on the main enemy of learning--fear. If you can abandon fear of failure, there is nowhere you will not explore; there is nothing you will not dare to learn; there is nothing you won't try. What is more, any mistakes that do happen can be dealt with--not only dealt with, but learned from. A samurai doesn't seek mistakes, but neither does he/she fear them. On the contrary, a samurai wears every mistake they have made like a badge of honor, because each one is a crisis which they have dug themself out from under; and each was a valuable lesson learned.

1.3.1.1.3 Colleagues

"To treat a person harshly is the way of middle class lackeys."

No matter your career, you will need to deal with people, at some point. It may be a highly social job, such as sales, or you may run an internet business from your basement. In all cases, there will

Instruction Manual for the 21st Century Samurai

1.3.1.1 Career

eventually be a time when you need to socialize. So when that time comes and you find yourself interacting, on the job, how do you behave in such a way that would do a samurai proud? It's been said that the true attitude of the samurai goes against the common stereotypes people often have of the brutal, macho warrior classes. Nowhere is this more apparent than in Yamamoto's views on how to treat your colleagues. As the above quote clearly states, Yamamoto saw harsh treatment as a kind of social vulgarity that was beneath a samurai's dignity and self-mastery.

Quotes such as "be intimate with all one's comrades" and "praise his good points and use every device to encourage him" further bring home how deeply Yamamoto believed in the samurai's duty to get along with his/her colleagues. Even the rough and tumble Ronin, Miyamoto, believed it was necessary for a leader to "take into account the abilities and limitations of his men, circulating among them and asking nothing unreasonable. He should know their morale and encourage them when necessary. This is the same as the principle of strategy." This shows how prevalent this view was, among samurai. There is, it seems, an implication that it is a sign of weakness not to be able to "handle" other people in a skillful, even-handed and dignified way--a way that demonstrated a warrior's discipline, power and grace.

So, what is the samurai solution to dealing with colleagues? A samurai sees teamwork, on the job, as the ultimate duty of the warrior. An employee or a leader who cannot control their anger, jealousy, etc., and therefore cannot be civil to their coworkers is, in the samurai view, not self-disciplined enough to be called a warrior. Take good relations with your colleagues as a personal challenge. Are you enough of a warrior to master your baser emotions and "handle" anyone with enough skill to befriend them? If you can, then you are a truly dedicated warrior, who Yamamoto himself may have welcomed into his clan.

Instruction Manual for the 21st Century Samurai

1.3.1.2 Dreams

If you are reading this book, you are already a dreamer. And welcome to the club. No one picks up a book about how to live as a samurai without being a first-class dreamer. For that matter, no one writes such a book without, also, having had his heads in the clouds at some point. Dreams and aspirations are what makes life exciting, hopeful and fun. So how should a samurai dream? What does a samurai envision, when their head rises up into the clouds? How do we dream like a samurai?

It is possible, when reading the works of the masters, to see the kinds of dreams and aspirations that may've appealed to the samurai. We can also see what kind of things they were not interested in. Yamamoto states that "riches and honors" are the two things that can most easily "blemish" a samurai. He further says that if a samurai stays in "strained circumstances, he will not be marred." So clearly, money and fame aren't the kind of thing that samurai dream about.

But before you put this book down, hoping for a little fame and fortune in your future, note that a samurai doesn't necessarily want to be a nobody with an empty bank account. The samurai ethic is merely to live simply. Spartanism is very much the style of the samurai class. You can have a few houses, a full bank account and a fan base and still be a samurai. Just be sure, when you are sitting in one of those houses, that you have simple, practical furniture; simple, practical food and that you generally keep yourself firm and tempered by avoiding excessive comforts.

In other words, a samurai does not seek poverty. Far from it, those in poverty cannot lead armies. After a samurai won a battle, their lord would reward them with fiefs and titles. The key is not to be poor, but to not be spoiled by luxuries, and so soften your warrior's edge. A samurai is tempered like steel, not soft and pampered.

1.3.1.2 Dreams

So, now that we know not to wish for all the luxuries money can buy, what should we dream for? What would make a samurai happy? The works of the three masters reveal the secrets of what dreams motivated the samurai. They can be broken into these three areas: 1. Self-mastery, 2. Enlightenment, 3. Prowess. By examining these three motivations and examining the "samurai solutions", given by the masters, we can learn to have hopes and dreams worthy of a shogun.

1.3.1.2.1 Self-mastery

"The gods and Buddhas, too, first started with a vow."

The ultimate dream of the samurai, of course, is to craft themself into the perfect warrior. Creating a warrior code is no good if you lack the strength to follow it. Every samurai dreams of following their warrior path to the high point of perfection and that usually begins with a vow. Yamamoto said "if one dedicates these four vows to the gods and Buddhas every morning, he will have the strength of two men and will never slip backward. One must edge forward like the inchworm, bit by bit." He was speaking of the four vows of the Nabeshima warrior clan, which he recommended reciting, in a solemn ceremony, every morning. Miyamoto, too, had a similar idea in mind when he wrote, about his nine point code of conduct: "It is important to start by setting these broad principles in your heart, and train in the Way of strategy."

To both of these masters, starting your day with discipline and a solemn vow, before everything you consider sacred, was an essential ingredient to being a samurai. And sticking to the vow, day by day-- improving, as said, bit by bit, like an inch-worm--was the only way to self-mastery. So how do we learn to make vows like a samurai and master ourselves? What vows, exactly, did the masters make to reach their heights of warrior perfection?

Instruction Manual for the 21st Century Samurai

1.3.1.2 Dreams

The exact vows of the samurai are clearly left behind for us to follow. They can be divided into the widely known nine point "bushido code", Miyamoto's nine point "strategy code" and Yamamoto's four point "Nabeshima code". For our purposes, we will also include the all-important vow to come to terms with death. Yamamoto stated that "if by setting one's heart right every morning and evening, one is able to live as though his body were already dead, he gains freedom in the Way. His whole life will be without blame, and he will succeed in his calling." The point here is that the way of the samurai is in acceptance of death.

This is an idea taken from Zen Buddhism. The master monk, Dōgen, said something similar, when he wrote: "you are freed from birth-and-death and become Buddha." The individual codes can be read about in the chapters at the start of this book, titled "The Three Masters"(1.2). The scholarly or ambitious aspiring samurai is free to memorize them and make his/her vows using every one of the codes. But, because this book is designed for quick reference-- and for the most battle-ready convenience--we will condense the codes into a shorter, more convenient form. We seek to learn from all three masters, in order to get an accurate overall education in the samurai lifestyle. To that purpose, we will combine these codes into one central code. Some of the ideas in the various codes overlap and repeat themselves. Some, in fact, though useful, are not absolutely essential to being a samurai.

So we will condense the most essential points of all codes into seven simple points. We will give this new code the simple but highly descriptive name, "modern samurai code." Because it is condensed from the genuine codes of the three masters, we can make our vows to this code, every morning, with full confidence that we are following a code worthy of the three samurai masters. The new code is as follows:

1. The way of the samurai is acceptance of death and impermanence.

1.3.1.2 Dreams

2. The way of the samurai is in trust and honesty.
3. The way of the samurai is in compassion and peace.
4. The way of the samurai is loyalty to friends and family.
5. The way of the samurai is to be fearless and self-sufficient.
6. The way of the samurai is to be civilized and of spotless reputation.
7. The way of the samurai is to abandon self-interest and devote oneself to the lord.

(Please note this need not mean a real "lord." It could be a real employer or boss. But "lord" could also be--symbolically--a spouse, a child, a religion, an ideal or anything you may wish to devote yourself to.)

So what is the samurai solution to self-mastery? This answer is clearer than most. It is to follow our "modern samurai code". By vowing to uphold this code, every morning, in a solemn ceremony, we can start our day like the samurai did; we can pledge the vows of the three greatest samurai masters, combined, and so have access to the most concentrated techniques of samurai self-mastery.

1.3.1.2.2 Enlightenment

"Negotiate the Way in zazen under the guidance of a true teacher and gain complete realization of the Buddha…"

The samurai were a spiritual class and theirs was a very practical brand of spirituality. Unlike the medieval knights of Europe, who often lived by Christian precepts and later by a code of chivalry, the samurai did more than just stick to their warrior codes. By practicing zazen, the practice of constant, never-ending meditation, the dedicated samurai lived every moment within their religion. Because enlightenment offered liberation from fear and worldly cares--and therefore made it easier to follow the stringent codes of bushido--every true samurai had the ambition to become fully proficient at zazen and thus reach the blissful freedom of enlightenment. Dōgen, the veritable founding father of Zen and

Instruction Manual for the 21st Century Samurai

1.3.1.2 Dreams

zazen in Japan, can offer us the best insight into how the samurai could achieve this lofty dream.

Zazen is, of course, a profound thing. But Dōgen sums it up in the chapter of his work called "Bendowa". Dōgen states: "There is an extremely easy way to become Buddha. If you refrain from all evil, do not cling to birth-and-death; work in deep compassion for all sentient beings, respecting those over you and showing compassion for those below you, without detesting or desiring, worrying or lamentation--that is Buddhahood."

These are all things which an aspiring Buddha could ponder, individually, and so come closer to enlightenment. If you consciously tried to be all of the above things, you would already be practicing zazen. But Dōgen offered an even deeper path to zazen, for more advanced students. According to this deeper path, the good qualities mentioned above are merely the results of a change of perspective; they are the natural consequence of changing the way we look at reality. It is simple to say "perceive the oneness of all things" but it is difficult to do this, practically. You can understand it, intellectually, but to actually "see" it and alter your perspective of all things is a very difficult thing to attain. But if you could do this, Dōgen states, you would naturally repel evil, live for all things, etc.

It is good to try to stick to the moral precepts contained in the above quote, but by understanding and living Dōgen's ideas of "oneness" you would fully understand, on a gut level, exactly why the above precepts are the only logical ways to behave, given the true nature of reality. Dōgen offered a way to understand how this oneness exists by perceiving the fact that everything, without exception, is made of "time" or what he called "uji". It is not easy to comprehend the nature of "uji", so do not be discouraged if you cannot grasp it at first reading. But if you can, eventually, come to understand what the master means by "uji", you will have graduated to the understanding of a more advanced form of zazen.

1.3.1.2 Dreams

"We must see the various things of the whole world as so many times. These things do not get in each other's way any more than various times get in each other's way. Because of this, there is an arising of the religious mind at the same time, and it is the arising of time of the same mind. So it is with practice and attainment the Way. We set our self out in array, and we see that. Such is the fundamental reason of the Way--that our self is time."

This is all very profound. But such is the challenge to the aspiring samurai. So, just what is the samurai solution to attaining the dream of enlightenment? Simply, to learn to practice zazen. By studying the words above, some insight into Zen and zazen can be gleaned, but monks in monasteries spend years or decades attaining a full mastery of these principles. So, it is recommended for the aspiring samurai to spend a little of their free time reading all of Dōgen's work and that of all the other Zen masters. Read the Zen koans, which are small parables meant to aid in enlightenment. Find a Bodhi tree(or the nearest available equivalent), read the koans and lead your mind ever deeper into an understanding of zazen. Eventually, you can make zazen your perpetual attitude to life. According to Dōgen, this is all you need to become enlightened. As Dōgen put it: "Do not search beyond it."

1.3.1.2.3 Prowess

"The Way is in the training."

Miyamoto was known far and wide for his prowess as a swordsman. As a young man, his dream was to be a famous samurai warrior--the best duelist in Japan! His dream came true and by the time he died, he was already considered the greatest warrior in Japan. So how did he do it? One major dream of the samurai is the desire to gain incredible skill with our weaponry and fighting style; to gain legendary prowess as a warrior. We can learn a lot from Miyamoto about how to go about doing this. Gaining prowess could literally mean taking martial arts classes and developing a genuine martial

1.3.1.2 Dreams

prowess--like the samurai of old. But it could be applied to practically any other art or discipline, as well. It could be applied to your painting career; to your sous chef career; to your amateur rugby career. Prowess is not strictly a martial thing. Prowess can be gained in any area where we wish to acquire true mastery. So what were Miyamoto's secrets? How did he gain his legendary prowess as a samurai warrior?

Miyamoto may have been a rough and tumble ronin, but he had a very spiritual and arcane philosophy of life. His main explanation for his prowess was his understanding of what he called "strategy". This kind of strategy was actually something very deep and intuitive. Miyamoto himself said that he "cannot write in detail how this is done" because it was something he understood intrinsically and could not easily be put into words. But, as it turns out, he did a good enough job for us to understand it and to further explain it here. This strategy can be summed up in the quote "from one thing, know ten thousand things."

That is easier said than done, but Miyamoto was able to do it because he developed what he called "intuitive judgment". He had studied the sword so well, he could make snap judgments about his opponent's movements and be correct; he could make a quick choice about where to move his sword and be spot on. This is why Miyamoto told his students of the Niten-ryū school to learn all arts and professions. In the "ground book", Miyamoto devoted quite some time to explaining the ways in which a foreman carpenter's job was similar to that of a samurai commander. All of life's disciplines have something in common, or some pearl of knowledge that can be applied to other disciplines.

So, the more areas of life you can develop intuitive judgment within, the more you can improve your overall powers of judgment. In addition, if you have enemies standing in the way between you and

Instruction Manual for the 21st Century Samurai

1.3.1.2 Dreams

glory, intuitive judgment can help you to best them, and so gain prowess in your field. Whether on the rugby field, the judo mat or that big-time international sous chef competition, having intuitive judgment can be the key to coming out on top. Miyamoto also said: "If you master the principles of sword-fencing, when you freely beat one man, you beat any man in the world. The spirit of defeating a man is the same for ten million men." For precise instructions on the strategies Miyamoto used to fight his enemies, see the chapter titled "strategy"(1.3.1.7.3).

So what is the samurai solution to developing prowess? This answer is a little more profound and difficult to understand than most. Miyamoto suggests you develop "intuitive judgment" which will allow you to always make the best choice in the quickest possible way. How do you develop intuitive judgment? Practice, study and more practice. Miyamoto said "The Way is in the training." Meaning that only by getting to know your art inside out, and as many related arts and trades, can you develop the intuitive judgment necessary to gain real prowess as a warrior (or as anything else you may strive to be). The samurai solution to prowess is not an easy one to follow. It takes a lot of practice, dedication and the ability to understand Miyamoto's very profound idea of "strategy". But if developing prowess were easy, then we would all be like Musashi Miyamoto. It is not easy to become the best in our field, but thanks to Miyamoto, we can at least have the samurai solution to give us the competitive edge.

Instruction Manual for the 21st Century Samurai

1.3.1.3 Love

"A samurai's word is harder than metal."

Although warriors first, the samurai were also the absolute essence of loyalty. In matters of love, concepts like fidelity, unselfish service and trust were the watchwords. These things may seem simple, but how much of this exists, truly, in the average modern relationship? Far from being the norm, among the modern lover's ethic, these things are seen as rarities; that Holy Grail, which heart-broken lovers, around the world, are searching for in vain.

Although the three masters didn't spend much time teaching their students about romance, there is actually a large amount of relevant wisdom to be found in the samurai outlook, which we can apply to creating an enduring relationship. So, how does a samurai love? What does a samurai seek in a lover and what kind of love does he/she give in return?

Yamatomo had the most to say, which is applicable to love and relationships. His experience in the palace courts gave him a better feeling for the intricacies of personal relationships and how a samurai should deal with them. The warrior principles that best apply to the realm of love are: 1. Devotion, 2. Compassion and 3. Respect.

1.3.1.3.1 Devotion

"Earnestly esteem one's master."

Samurai fell in love, just like anybody else. And when they did, they likely tried to reconcile their feelings for their adored one with the principles of the bushido code. As stated in our "modern samurai code"(1.3.1.2.1), one of the ways of the samurai is to "abandon self-interest and devote oneself to the lord." In our modern age, none

1.3.1.3 Love

of us serve under an actual feudal lord, but this principle can be applied to a spouse, a child, a boss, an ideal or anything else we wish to devote ourselves to. The only important element here is that the samurai's way is one of selfless service. This is, of course, very applicable to love and relationships. It is likely that when the samurai of old fell in love, they applied their newfound feelings to the bushido principle of "Loyalty." In other words, "be an example of trust." That, mixed with the samurai ethic of selfless dedication makes for the perfect lover.

An entirely trustworthy lover, who is selflessly devoted to the object of their affection? What more could anyone ask for? A samurai, given they are a true samurai, makes just such an ideal lover. But you may second guess how ideal this situation is. We all know people out there who are selflessly devoted to a lover that exploits and uses them; a lover who takes, takes, takes and never gives anything back. How does an adoring samurai avoid such a situation?

It is to be hoped the object of the samurai's affection will appreciate the vast amount of love and devotion they are receiving. If they don't, the samurai will likely stick around longer than most, until they do. All the samurai really needs, in love, is a partner that appreciates all they're willing to give. But, as a final point, Yamamoto said that it is better to avoid getting to know those "about whom you have formerly had some doubts." It is better to avoid potentially dangerous friendships. For all those worried your dedicated heart may be taken advantage of, Yamamoto's reminder is recommended.

So what is the samurai solution to romantic devotion? Samurai were all about service, it is true, but they chose their lord wisely. They did this for a good reason. Once you pledge service, you are in it for the long haul. A samurai will stick with you to the end. But, in spite of that, the end can sometimes come in the form of a realization that love has died--in which case, the battle is lost. It may be hard to

Instruction Manual for the 21st Century Samurai

1.3.1.3 Love

leave the one you love, but when the battle is lost, a samurai will move on. It may seem harsh, but yours is a hard and disciplined path. Being a samurai is all about selfless service and if the lord abuses the servant, it is no longer a situation of service; it becomes the situation of a victim. It is never acceptable for a samurai to be a victim. It is never acceptable to allow a lord to abuse you or rob you of your dignity. In such a situation, it is acceptable to walk away.

1.3.1.3.2 Compassion

"Work in deep compassion for all sentient beings."

Dōgen, Yamamoto and Miyamoto all stressed the importance of compassion. It may seem paradoxical when you consider the role of a warrior is to defeat enemies on the battlefield. But Yamamoto, himself--that ancestor of ruthless and renowned military commanders--put it best when he said: "a person of little merit is not at peace but walks about making trouble and is in conflict with all." Put another way, "a samurai causes no conflict."

It is not only our duty to develop an over-arching compassion for all living things, as a part of our enlightenment, but it is particularly important to do so with our lover. This means that our compassion would never allow us to do anything that would threaten the well-being of our loved one. What is the samurai solution here? In order for our relationship to be of true samurai caliber, we must develop and retain a strong and enduring preoccupation with the welfare of our partner.

This is a simple point, but all-important. Our spouse or lover is the perfect person upon which to practice our zazen sense of compassion. As you practice zazen and come to feel an ever growing compassion, the first recipient of that compassion should be your partner. They are the closest to you and the most ready and receptive vessel to receive your new understanding of love and compassion. Compassion is the samurai way, in general, and so it

1.3.1.3 Love

follows any true samurai's relationship would a loving, gentle and sensitive bond. This applies to relationships that are thriving and going strong, and also to those which may have become estranged. In all things, you must make a sincere attempt to be compassionate.

1.3.1.3.3 Respect

If you're looking for "a little respect" then look no further than the nearest samurai. Contrary to the stereotypes of the brutish, sword-wielding barbarians, the samurai were a genteel example of the warrior class. A brigand or petty swordsman may treat their spouse with contempt, but not a samurai.

Given what we know of the samurai codes, it would be a matter of the deepest disgrace to abuse someone to whom we have pledged our devotion and love. That alone would be a violation of our word--something particularly abhorrent to a samurai. This disgrace would be compounded if the lover that we victimize is weaker than ourselves or, at the very least, not a samurai of similar prowess. All these things are in conflict with a samurai's sense of honor and so, naturally, that puts the kibosh on disrespectful behavior to the spouse, as far as samurai went. Just as in our modern world, it is only the smallest and basest type of person who abuses their family and samurai were the antithesis of this type of person. Not only would they not behave this way, they would abhor and challenge those who do.

To demonstrate the truth of this, Yamamoto had some very specific pieces of advice on respectful social behavior, which certainly applied to a spouse or lover as much as to anyone else. They are many and varied, but the samurai way of respecting a spouse can be summed up in the following four quotes:

1. "It is because a samurai has correct manners, that he is admired." A samurai may have high ideals for himself/herself, but they are

Instruction Manual for the 21st Century Samurai

1.3.1.3 Love

accepting of the flaws of others--including their spouse. You can yell at them all you like; they won't yell back. They will be polite in return and accepting of your flaws. By doing this, they will build the trust in your relationship, until it is strong and enduring. Samurai are particularly accepting of others and are geared towards selfless service, in general. So, if you want a lover that will stick by you, and help support you through the rough patches, your samurai lover is the natural choice. Now, you may see potential for an inconsiderate lover to exploit the samurai. For reasons why this is unlikely, see the section titled "Devotion"(1.3.1.3.1).

2. "Meet people cordially at all times and without distraction."
Similar to the quote, "one should look his listener in the eye", this demonstrates the samurai ethic of affording full respect to the people you engage with, by giving them your full attention. With a lover, in particular, this is an often overlooked essential to a good relationship. Full, dedicated attention; a heartfelt smile and a sincere desire to communicate--this is a simple solution to a lot of the seemingly complex problems that can develop in a relationship.

3. "Lies and insincerity are unbecoming. This is because they are for self-profit."
Yamamoto disapproved of lies, if they are selfish. They go against the samurai ideal of nurturing trust. But, it would come as a surprise to many that he considered it acceptable to lie or commit the sin of omission if it is for genuinely selfless or even charitable reasons. For example, if a spouse is sick and looking haggard, it is acceptable to tell your spouse they're looking beautiful. An enlightened samurai, in any case, should be able to see beyond physical beauty and into the beauty of the soul--so, in fact, this may not be a lie. But this should give you an idea of the type of "white lies" samurai may tell.

4. "Inside the skin of a dog, outside the hide of a tiger."
Lastly, a samurai cares about appearance. He/she doesn't much care how others look, being accepting of others, in general. But matters

1.3.1.3 Love

of personal appearance and hygiene are paramount in the samurai's mind. It is seen as a form of respect, similar to looking your spouse in the eye when you speak or avoiding selfish deceptions. "Skin of a dog" refers to the samurai's internal lack of luxury--needing only a place to sleep and a simple meal, in the best spartan traditions. But "hide of a tiger" demonstrates that, in spite of their internal simplicity, it is a samurai's duty to look sharp. Far from being a matter of vanity and ego, this wish to look good is nothing more than an extension of the samurai ethic of service. It is a matter of etiquette, as well as a matter of reflecting well on the dignity of the samurai class.

So what is the samurai solution to showing respect for our partner? 1. Be polite and non-judgmental, 2. Give your time and attention, 3. Don't be deceptive and 4. Don't neglect your appearance. These points sound simple, but respect is the under-rated bedrock of any good relationship and, if followed to the letter, could well help create a relationship as lofty and enduring as the most celebrated samurai legend.

Instruction Manual for the 21st Century Samurai

1.3.1.4 Children

"Even the birds and beasts are
affected by what they are used
to seeing and hearing from the
time they are born."

Yamamoto believed that loving
parents were strongly preferred in order to bring up strong samurai
children. This encouraged familial loyalty in the child and so helped
them to more effortlessly fulfill part of the samurai code. But,
besides that, Yamamoto had a surprising amount to say about the
proper raising of children. One doesn't think of samurai warriors as
being big on child-rearing tips, but keep in mind this was a very
genteel and refined class of warrior. Miyamoto, that tough-as-nails
fighter of legendary renown, said the way of the warrior is the
"twofold Way of pen and the sword, and he should have a taste for
both Ways." This meant that learning and broad knowledge was as
much a samurai duty as was mastering of the martial arts. So, how
did samurai parents raise their children to be able warriors?
Yamamoto had the most to say about this, but the views of Dōgen
and Miyamoto can also apply. The insights of the masters,
concerning child-rearing can be divided into 1. Discipline, 2. Setting
an example and 3. Nurturing.

1.3.1.4.1 Discipline

"It is a mistake for parents to thoughtlessly make their children
dread…"

Contrary to what many people would expect of fierce fighters from
back in the mists of a harsher, crueler past, samurai parents did not
believe in corporal punishment. The reasons were many, but most
importantly, Yamamoto suggested that a child who is taught to live
in fear could not easily become bold, in later life. Dealing with
children severely, basically, condemns them to a life of shrinking
submissiveness, which is incompatible with the life and outlook of a

1.3.1.4 Children

warrior. As Yamamoto put it: "If a person is affected by cowardice as a child, it remains a lifetime scar." It was thought that harsh treatment encouraged fear and a tendency to cowardice. It is, of course, possible for a child to develop bravery after such treatment, but it is much harder for them, and there is no guarantee they will not be permanently cowed. Warriors must learn to endure hardship, but not until they are adults!

Warrior children are more likely to sprout from out of a soil which is safe, comfortable and free of fear. Far from advising parents to physically punish their children, Yamamoto clearly stated that "a child will become timid if he is scolded severely." There seems to be a suggestion that such brutish and bullying behavior is beneath the dignity and quality of character of a samurai. After all, Yamamoto said that "to treat a person harshly is the way of middle class lackeys" and this maxim no doubt applies to children as much as to adults--if not more so. It may be acceptable for lackeys, brigands or unskilled swordsmen to mistreat their children but, by the samurai estimate, it is a small person, indeed, who would direct their formidable samurai powers against a weak and defenseless child. Such a low act would not only be unacceptable, but would no doubt be source of great shame and personal disgrace.

So what is the samurai solution to disciplining children? The same that applies to treatment of other people, applies to children. Yamamoto said, "it is because a samurai has correct manners, that he is admired" and there is no reason for children to be an exception to that rule. It is okay to direct and exert a powerful influence on your children. In fact, you should take a very energetic role in directing and guiding their activities, to assure they grow up to be samurai, and not something else. But the usual standard of punishing children is very incompatible with the samurai ethic. Yamamoto did say punishment and rewards were acceptable, in some cases, but harsh treatment is not the samurai way. Remember that a samurai is enlightened and therefore compassionate. As a result, talking to your child and identifying their troubles, with a

Instruction Manual for the 21st Century Samurai

1.3.1.4 Children

genuine, compassionate concern for their well-being is far more in keeping with the samurai outlook. This is much harder than simply punishing. But the samurai thrives on taking the more difficult path; the samurai strives to be a cut above the rest, in child-rearing, as in anything else. Rather than the commonly employed punishment and rewards methods, see the chapters titled "Setting an example" (1.3.1.4.2) and "Nurturing"(1.3.1.4.3) for specific advice on samurai methods of raising strong warrior children.

1.3.1.4.2 Setting an example

"Let him not know avarice."

Nowadays it has become conventional wisdom that children will do as their parents do, not as they say. But, long ago, it was already a part of the samurai strategy of child-rearing. Yamamoto warned against teaching avarice, but from his writing, it can be inferred that he believed in setting an example for your children, in all things. Your children cannot expect to behave to a standard of virtue that you, yourself, are incapable of attaining. This is a component of upbringing that is often underestimated, these days.

Simply being a good example will take care of most of the character-building you may want of your child and it is perhaps the largest part of the samurai strategy of child-rearing. This may sound simple, but how many parents, nowadays, live by the high and lofty standards of the samurai? Modern society encourages no particular standard and, as a result, most of us do not consider it particularly important to improve our character or eliminate our faults.

That lackadaisical attitude to self-mastery may well be reflected in the amount of problems the modern family has, with their children. Children learn all the bad habits of the parents and are naturally

1.3.1.4 Children

indignant when they are expected to behave better than their parents do. This obliterates trust and confidence in the parent's claim to authority, especially during the rebellious teen years; relations break down and, before long, conflicts arise. The average parent will know of no way to respond to this conflict, except with threats of punishment. This confrontational attitude often causes further alienation, distrust and disrespect. Given a samurai tries to set an example, they can avoid teaching their children their faults in the first place and would not expect them to be more virtuous than they are--hence, this kind of relationship breakdown may well be avoided. Perhaps it would not always be the case, but it is certainly much more likely to be avoided. When mixed with the samurai ethic of non-punishment and compassionate nurturing, the likelihood of this kind of collapse of the family unit is far less. A samurai family unit is likely to be a stable alliance.

So, what is the samurai solution to raising children? Mostly, to set an example. Again, this sounds very basic, but it is far more profound when you consider how extremely rare such a parenting method is, in fact, in our modern society. The prevalent method, at least in the west, is punishment and rewards--very few alternatives to that are expounded by the average parent. But we are samurai parents--as in all things, we seek to take the harder path, which wields more than average results. In all areas of striving, we strive to elevate ourselves to the lofty levels of the three masters, including in the area of child-rearing. Given that merely setting an example is central to the samurai method, then by following the precepts of this book and developing ourselves as warriors, we are already setting an example and doing most of what is required to successfully raise warrior children. To complete the picture of how a samurai raises children, please see the chapter titled "Nurturing" (1.3.1.4.3).

1.3.1.4.3 Nurturing

"Fixedness means a dead hand. Pliability is a living hand."

Instruction Manual for the 21st Century Samurai

1.3.1.4 Children

Miyamoto was talking about his fighting strategy and the way one should grip their weapons, in the above quote. But it corresponds with a lot of Yamamoto's ideas of parenthood and with the general ideas of compassion and service, which defines the samurai outlook on life. This outlook, of course, applies to children as well. Samurai did not raise children with a firm hand, but with a pliable one. In our "modern samurai code"(1.3.1.2.1) we know that the way of the samurai is to "abandon self-interest and devote oneself to the lord." In this day and age, I don't think any of us will find ourselves serving in the army of an actual feudal lord, but this principle can be applied to our child, our spouse or anyone or anything that we wish to devote ourselves to. Samurai were all about selfless, flawless devotion. Service was one of their greatest passions.

The original meaning of the word samurai was "one who serves." The average person looks upon service as demeaning--as something reserved for the weak and servile. But the samurai does not serve because of weakness, but, rather, because of strength. The samurai serves with all the flawless ability of the tempered warrior. But they, and only they, choose the lord they will bestow their service on. So, this is not something they do because they are forced by a stronger party; this is something they do by choice and because only they are strong enough to do it. It is a source of pride and dignity, and the samurai have plenty of both.

Yamamoto said "a samurai's word is harder than metal." Any oath, promise or responsibility is taken extremely seriously. So, it stands to reason, if someone willingly takes on the responsibility of having a child, it is an absolute requirement to fulfill those obligations. A samurai is duty-bound not only to take care of the basic physical requirements of the child, but also to put in the time and attention to properly bring it up. It is advisable to approach it from the standpoint of our "modern samurai code" and to abandon self-interest and devote ourselves to our child, as we would a lord.
So what is the samurai solution to solving our children's problems? Devotion. Plain and simple, we should be as devoted to our child as

1.3.1.4 Children

a samurai to their lord. If we ponder this, the answers should come to us crystal clear. Yamamoto said "always give full attention to your listener" and "a samurai has correct manners". Taken in the context of your child this means you must give your child all the time and respectful attention as they need--it is your responsibility as their parent and as a samurai to take such responsibilities very seriously. In addition, when Miyamoto said "pliability is a living hand" he helped us to understand that we should give our pliable attention to the child, in order to serve and nurture with sensitivity and with an eye to helping them along their path of development. Children need a strong hand to hold; yours is stronger than most. Their welfare should be an abiding concern and there should be no lengths you would not go, to assure the child's needs are met. This is true devotion. What's more, developing compassion is another one of our duties and Dōgen specifically said that "showing compassion for those below you" is a sign of a Buddha. This should be done, and never in half measures. All these ways of treating children become obvious, if you understand what it means to treat a child as you would a lord.

You may imagine this would lead to a spoiled child, but keep in mind that you are not only raising children like a samurai, you are also raising a samurai child. You should be pliable and compassionate, but you should also be strictly dedicated to teaching them samurai ethics. The samurai temperament is not compatible with that of a spoiled child; so eventually, if you correctly wean your child onto the path of samurai ways, your child will outgrow their comfortable upbringing and will seek self-reliance. Remember also, you may be putting your child in the place of the lord but this does not mean your child controls you. This is no more true than it would be of a genuine feudal lord. Your service is voluntary; your service is borne of your endless well of strength; your service is your privilege and your reward. When added to the samurai ethic of non-punishment and setting a good example, true devotion assures it would take a very strong blow, indeed, to disrupt the secure and loving bonds of the samurai family.

Instruction Manual for the 21st Century Samurai

1.3.1.5 Death

"The Way of the warrior is resolute acceptance of death."

One thing is certain, the ability to come to terms with death is one of the all-time hallmarks of the samurai warrior and put them a cut above the rest of history's warrior classes. The ability to rise above the fear of death may well have been a common feature of history's best fighters, but in no class was the art of accepting death more fully ingrained than it was among the samurai. In addition to the above quote, by Miyamoto, Yamamoto said "The Way of the Samurai is found in death" and Dōgen attributed Buddha-like greatness to those who "do not cling to birth-and-death". And so, all three masters were in solid agreement on this matter. But how did the samurai go about learning to accept death?

Yamamoto saw life as a "marionette show" ; one big illusion, lacking reality, and it seems this attitude helped him to avoid attachment to life and the material things that it offers.

Buddhist philosophy often takes the identical viewpoint, calling the earth a place of "maya", meaning "illusion". Being such a major component of the samurai outlook, all three masters had something to say about death. The wisdom of the masters can be divided into three areas: 1. Our death, 2. Other's death, 3. Impermanence

1.3.1.5.1 Our death

"Death is considered loss and life is considered gain. Thus, death is something that such a person does not care for, and he is contemptible."

Yamamoto sums up the view of the samurai, considering how they should view the inevitable event of their own death. We should be able to look past it; not be particularly bothered about it. Only with

Instruction Manual for the 21st Century Samurai

1.3.1.5 Death

that attitude could a warrior jump into the fray and fight with the kind of fearlessness that wins battles. Remember, our mantra, as a samurai, is selfless service.

Whereas Yamamoto says that contemptible people use loss and gain as their compass, a samurai uses the warrior codes as their compass. The codes tell us to abandon self-interest and serve our lord. We pay far less attention to the possibility of our own death, therefore, than we do to the preserving of other's lives. We are the only ones strong enough to fill that all-important protective role and therefore it is our privilege to abandon self-interest.

So what is the samurai solution to coming to terms with our death? As said in the opening of this chapter, Yamamoto saw life as a "marionette show". By this, he meant that life is illusory and the material things that we so value, here on earth, don't actually have the value they seem to have. Naturally, if you could come to fully believe this, you would have little difficulty abandoning life's material pleasures and consequently would have far less attachment to life and less fear of death. This is a very Buddhist concept, which proves Yamamoto's dedication to Zen. According to the monk, Dōgen, many are held back from enlightenment by this "marionette show" or, as he describes them, the "worldly people lost in samsara (the physical world of death and rebirth)". This basically restates what Yamamoto says and brings home the final word on the samurai solution to death, which, basically, is to always be aware of the delusory nature of the material world and lessen your attachment to life by gaining enlightenment. For further help on this topic, see the chapter titled enlightenment"(1.3.1.2.2).

1.3.1.5.2 Other's death

"When you would see into a person's heart, become ill."

We will all be in a situation where someone we know will become

Instruction Manual for the 21st Century Samurai

1.3.1.5 Death

sick--even to the point of being on death's door. How do you respond to that situation?

An amazing amount of "friends" will do their best to avoid the sickbed. Whether it is because they find illness depressing or because they are afraid it's contagious or because they are "fair weather friends", Yamamoto was saying that you don't really know who your friends are until you are sick, dying or, in some other way, between a rock and a hard place.

So what is the samurai solution to a sick or dying friend? We must pay our respects. We would even go so far as to say we must express our reverence. Death is not only something we must reconcile with, personally. It is also something we have to come to friendly terms with, concerning the ones we love. Of course, just like anyone, we lament the loss of a loved-one. The difference is, we will not avoid death or the dying; we are reconciled with the idea and will show our acceptance and reverence for life and death by never avoiding either. We must not be scared of death or the dying. If they are family, we are duty-bound to be at hand during their hardships--that is a component of "filial piety" or giving due respect and loyalty to our family. In addition, if it is a friend to whom we owe a debt, we should keep Yamamoto's words in mind: "you should never in your whole life be negligent toward someone from whom you have received a favor." A samurai always pays off a debt and always returns kind friendship with kind friendship. To sum up, a samurai is there for a friend in their time of need. To neglect your duties, in death, is just as bad as neglecting your duties, in life.

1.3.1.5.3 Impermanence

"Permanence is, in fact, the mind dividing up all things into good or bad."

In Dōgen's chapter on "Buddha nature", he offers this quote to help us understand that an enlightened person avoids seeing

1.3.1.5 Death

anything as permanent. It is part of enlightenment to understand the impermanence of things and, much like death, to come to terms with this state of things. But Dōgen is offering us an even deeper understanding of this, because he is stating that our labeling and judgment of things as being good or bad is what tempts us to want permanence.

For example, if you love someone, you want them with you forever. If you hate something, you want to get rid of it, for good. If we didn't form these good or bad opinions, we would have absolutely no need for permanence. Even the labelling of death as bad and life as good accounts for our wish to live forever and our fear of death.

So, what is the samurai solution to dealing with change? It is a very "Zen" solution. Our "modern samurai code"(1.3.1.2.1), states that one of the ways of the samurai is "acceptance of death". By extension, our duty as a samurai is to understand Zen Buddhism and to learn to accept not only death, but all of the inevitable changes of this very impermanent thing we call life. Dōgen gives us the best advice on how to do this practically. A samurai should try not to label the people and things of the material world as "good" or "bad", and in this way he/she can have the proper "Zen" outlook, as befits the traditional samurai. This doesn't mean we should avoid loving people, as compassion is another Buddhist concept we must remember--which encourages love.

Enlightenment is hard to grasp, but it is helpful to point out that enlightenment doesn't teach us not to love, but teaches how it is possible to love, universally, not just exclusively. With enlightenment, love and hate weaken and vanish; oneness obscures all boundaries and labels. It is only these labels that make us scared of change.

Instruction Manual for the 21st Century Samurai

1.3.1.6 Spiritual

"Every morning one should first do reverence to his master and parents and then to his patron deities and guardian Buddhas."

It has already been said in the chapter titled "self-mastery" that our samurai masters recommended a morning ceremony to pledge our devotion to the samurai codes. Well, on top of that, Yamamoto and Miyamoto also recommended including our parents, family, Buddhas and patron deities to that mix. In the chapter titled "family"(1.3.1.8) we can see that samurai believed strongly in the Confucian ideal of "filial piety" or loyalty to one's family. Although the samurai's main spiritual impetus was Zen Buddhism, there were many influences on the samurai's spiritual world. All the major religions of Asia, during that period of history, had some part in their spiritual outlook. The ideals of the Chinese philosopher Confucius figured into their view of family; the philosophical underpinnings of Chinese Taoism influenced their views of Yin/Yang, martial arts and the five elements; and the indigenous religion of Japan, the animistic Shinto, caused many samurai to select a patron deity or nature spirit for worship.

Given all this complexity, what can we consider the definitive definition of how the samurai worshipped? How can we define their spirituality? In this case, I think it is best to simplify. Although this subject is complex, for our purposes we can focus merely on the following three areas of spirituality and provide short, simple answers on how the aspiring modern samurai can approach their spiritual life. We will focus on the following three areas of samurai spirituality: 1. Deities, 2. Mysteries, 3. Cosmology.

1.3.1.6.1 Deities

"One should be in harmony his family gods."

Instruction Manual for the 21st Century Samurai

1.3.1.6 Spiritual

The samurai viewpoint was very connected to the indigenous Japanese religion, Shinto. A deeply spiritual religion, Shinto had a multitude of local Gods and spirits, which were often worshipped or feared by local peoples.

The samurai spiritual temperament was very influenced by Shinto and so it would not have been uncommon for a samurai to pay his/her respects at a Buddhist temple and then go to the local Shinto shrine to pray to the local nature spirit of their home district. Such a mixture of religions was not seen as contradictory, but rather, a unique feature of the Japanese spiritual character.

Miyamoto, in the introduction to the Book of Five Rings, said "I have climbed mountain Iwato of Higo in Kyushu to pay homage to Ten(Shinto heaven), pray to Kwannon(Buddhist goddess of mercy), and kneel before Buddha." This demonstrates the variety of influences that composed the samurai spiritual universe. Miyamoto clearly worshipped both Shinto and Buddhist gods and yet he famously said: "Respect Buddha and the gods without counting on their help." By this he did not mean that gods and Buddhas do not have powers, in his view, but rather that a samurai's mantra is self-sufficiency and self-mastery. It may be acceptable to pray to a deity for guidance, wisdom or even protection, but a samurai should not expect all his battles to be fought by deities--a samurai prides him / herself on their ability to win battles without, necessarily, being given any help. This applies to battles and, also, to life in general.

Yamamoto, of course, also expressed a belief in the powers of the gods and recommended a samurai pay respect to deities. Although to Yamamoto, it was of first importance to pay homage to the samurai codes and to your master. He seemed to believe that if you serve your master and your codes in the proper samurai fashion, everything else will sort itself out. As he put it:
"If he will only make his master first in importance, his parents will rejoice and the gods and Buddhas will give their assent."

1.3.1.6 Spiritual

So, in his different way, Yamamoto also believed in respecting the gods, but not directly petitioning them for rescue.

So what is the samurai solution to dealing with the gods? Miyamoto sums it up best in his quote: "Respect Buddha and the gods without counting on their help." In their different ways, both Yamamoto and Miyamoto said something along the lines that if a samurai fulfils the obligations of his/her code and lives the proper samurai life, with full courage and character, the gods will naturally bless them. In other words, they did not consider it appropriate to petition the gods through begging; in true warrior form, they believed in acquiring blessings through merit. In their view, the gods would naturally seek to bless a samurai who is genuinely committed and pure of heart. But if they didn't? Oh well. A samurai would not have relied on it, regardless. This is a very "que sera" way of petitioning the gods, but the samurai believe in being ready for anything and adaptable to any circumstance. So, although they would like the blessing of their deities, their attitude was simply to do their best, pay their proper respects, and hope for the best.

1.3.1.6.2 Mysteries

"Perceive those things which cannot be seen."

The Shinto religion was one of many Kami(gods), and these entities were varied in their powers and their natures. Some Kami were beneficent and all-powerful, something like the Greek gods; some were dark and strictly local, such as an evil river spirit or an angry ghost that haunts a building. The Shinto notion of Kami was more of a broad definition than what English speakers understand, when they refer to "the gods". Because a kami could be like a god; like a demon; like a ghost; like a nature spirit. Even a given forest animal could actually be a Kami, such as the "Kitsune." The Kitsune were spirits who took the form of foxes. They had high intelligence,

1.3.1.6 Spiritual

magical ability and a habit of playing tricks on mortals. This variety shows how, in the Shinto view, the world was completely infused with spirits.

Being a very Japanese institution, the samurai were very influenced by Japan's indigenous Shinto religion and so, it is a given they believed in a hidden, spiritual world, were Kami interacted with mortal souls. The mysteries of occult knowledge, supernatural happenings and ghost stories were not looked down upon as silly folly, but would likely have been treated quite seriously by any samurai. But how did the samurai approach this hidden realm? What did they consider the appropriate stance to the occult?

Yamamoto was fond of telling stories to express his samurai ideals-- much like parables. His stories often had a supernatural element to them. The following example is typical of Yamamoto's occult tales:

"In China there was once a man who liked pictures of dragons, and his clothing and furnishings were all designed accordingly. His deep affection for dragons was brought to the attention of the dragon god, and one day a real dragon appeared before his window. It is said that he died of fright. He was probably a man who always spoke big words but acted differently when facing the real thing."

This parable is obviously warning aspiring samurai against the dangers of not living up to your own "big words." He was appealing to samurai to show responsibility and live up to the standard of bravery expected of a true warrior.

But even more so, Yamamoto's parable could well serve as an example of what stance he took towards the supernatural. He accepted the existence of mysteries; the existence of the gods and powers greater than human beings. He considered it necessary to pay proper respect to gods and the supernatural. But, much like the parable of the dragon god, a samurai should not fear the supernatural. Much like dealing with the worldly threats of men, a

Instruction Manual for the 21st Century Samurai

1.3.1.6 Spiritual

samurai walked the world without fear, and that included fear of the supernatural.

So what is the samurai solution to the supernatural? As may be derived from Yamamoto's dragon parable, the samurai should believe in the supernatural, but should not fear it and should not really consider it his/her province. Miyamoto famously said: "Respect the gods, but do not rely on them." Much like dealing with the gods, the samurai respected the supernatural. They did not ridicule those with occult beliefs. Given this, there is no conflict in a modern day samurai joining his or her local ghost hunting society. But in the end, a samurai prefers to focus on the power of their own sword.

1.3.1.6.3 Cosmology

"There may be places that are beyond the celestial worlds; beyond the world of ordinary human beings."

This quote, from Dōgen, goes to show the vast and complex universe in which the samurai lived. As can be seen from the chapter of this book titled "Gods"(1.3.1.6.1), the indigenous Shinto religion of Japan was one of many gods and supernatural beings, called Kami. This wealth of deities expresses well the way in which Shinto saw the world--almost all elements of nature had a patron Kami, and the world was a very spiritual place, as a result. The samurai spiritual make-up was manifold. It was not uncommon for samurai to worship both Japanese Kami and Buddhist saints. As a result, to understand how the samurai saw the universe, we must consider the cosmology of both Zen Buddhism and Shinto. So how did Buddhism see the universe? How did this mix with Shinto to make the samurai view of the universe?

In Shōbōgenzō, Dōgen said: "We give rise to the intention to realize

1.3.1.6 Spiritual

enlightenment even within the worlds of the hells, the hungry ghosts, the animals, and the asuras." Zen Buddhism has a belief in the universe that is based on reincarnation and spiritual development. Those whose souls are furthest from enlightenment live in a place that is translated as "hell". This is a place with no Buddhism, little chance of enlightenment and a place where enlightenment is not even particularly sought after. The realm of the "Hungry Ghosts"--or souls that long for enlightenment, but live in a plane where it is largely unavailable--is between hell and the world of animals. Although we live on the same physical plane as the animals, we, as humans, fall somewhere between the animals and the Asuras. The Asuras are powerful, god-like beings who, although not immortal, live for an incredibly long time and have powers and abilities that make humans appear small and insignificant.

Dōgen was stating, in his quote, that enlightenment can spontaneously come to any being on this scale of existence, although for humans and asuras it is easiest to find Buddhism and, therefore, enlightenment. When we examine this quote, as we have, it concisely sums up how Zen Buddhism sees the universe and all souls in existence. So how did this mix with the quintessential Japanese religion of Shinto? As can be read about in the chapter titled "Gods"(1.3.1.6.1), spirits, gods and demons were everywhere, in the Shinto outlook. As we've seen, there are already a variety of beings in Zen Buddhist cosmology. But to the Japanese samurai, there were even more, by far. Because the physical world contained not only humans and animals, but Kami of all kinds. Both Shinto and Buddhism held a belief in other worlds and beings on varying levels of existence and enlightenment.

The samurai had a healthy respect for all the myriad beings that made up their universe. Miyamoto famously said, "respect Buddha and the gods without counting on their help." This expresses well how Samurai approached the vast variety to be found in their cosmology. They strove for enlightenment, and liberation from rebirth in the myriad worlds, but they manifested a genuine respect

1.3.1.6 Spiritual

and compassion for all existent things, whether human, animal, kami or revengeful ghost.

Above all, the samurai focused on their own development and didn't spend too much time considering other beings. As Miyamoto said, a samurai should try to "not deviate even a little from the Way of the warrior." , if possible, and so should concentrate on their own self-mastery. But on top of that, a samurai practiced zazen. This meant understanding, at all times, what Dōgen meant when he instructed monks: "Work in deep compassion for all sentient beings." This, ultimately, was the main religious purpose of the samurai and so it expresses how they approached the endless variety of worlds and all the myriad variety of beings to be found in these worlds.

1.3.1.7 Conflict

"I do not know the way to defeat others, but the way to defeat myself."

This quote by Yamamoto gives the clearest, simplest description of the samurai method of defeating your enemy. Most of it involves self-mastery, self-discipline and the defeat of those weaknesses inside us, which would make us into fearful and spineless individuals, if we let them control us. A warrior is controlled by no one, involuntarily, especially not by their own weaknesses. Miyamoto also said, "you must never allow yourself to be lead around by the enemy. You must be the one to lead the enemy around." And this can be applied to the words of Yamamoto. Namely, that we will master ourselves; we will not allow ourselves to be led around by our flaws and faults any more than we would allow our enemies to do so.

So how did the samurai deal with aggressors? How did they cut down their enemies when conflicts arose? Chiefly by a mixture of self-mastery and strategy. Miyamoto--that peerless duelist and swordsman--is the best source of advice, concerning conflict. Having bested Japan's best, during the height of Japan's warrior age, you can be confident Miyamoto's advice is perhaps the very best that could be given, concerning conflict and combat. The insights of the famous ronin can be divided into three areas: 1. Taking the high road, 2. Martial arts and 3. Strategy.

1.3.1.7.1 Taking the high road

"A samurai does not cause conflict."

The above quote, although not the exact words of Yamamoto, can be inferred from his words: "A person of little merit is not at peace

Instruction Manual for the 21st Century Samurai

1.3.1.7 Conflict

but walks about making trouble and is in conflict with all." Quite to the contrary of what most people would assume, samurai did not seek conflict. In fact, as this quote from Yamamoto demonstrates, it would be considered wrong to do so. Yamamoto was familiar with the ins and outs of "samurai manners" from his years in the palace and so we can be certain of his accuracy on this matter. Oh, they were very good at dealing with conflict--meeting an enemy squarely, with resolve and cutting them down in one quick stroke. For more on this topic, see the chapter titled "Strategy"(1.3.1.7.3). But they did not initiate conflict needlessly.

As a result of this aversion to violence, it would often be necessary for them to take the high road and ignore the crude words of people less refined and self-disciplined than themselves. It is true, samurai have pride and do not allow themselves to be debased, but would they always break out the sword at any hint of an indignity? The answer seems to be an emphatic no. There is a quote by Yamamoto, which says something along the lines that there is nothing wrong with allowing fools to think they are right. This implies that it is okay to walk away from uncultured or aggressive people, because, as we've learned, a samurai avoids conflict. In fact, much like "picking on" children or those weaker than us, it would be a source of shame to physically punish someone whose personality--in the samurai view--is no more advanced than a child. If we are dealing with a samurai of similar prowess and it is a personal challenge, then it is acceptable to meet insult with force. But when dealing with non-warriors, children, or those with--by samurai standards--crude, undeveloped personalities, it is the samurai's duty to walk away and avert the unnecessary bloodshed of a relatively defenceless individual.

So what is the samurai solution to being insulted by the ignorant? It is of the utmost priority to walk away, wherever possible. So long as there is no direct threat, then a samurai must abide by the precept that a samurai causes no conflict. Take it as a personal challenge, that your enlightenment and level of self-mastery allows for the

1.3.1.7 Conflict

nastiest of provocation to vanish harmlessly into the vast skies of your warrior composure. In other words, be the bigger man- -or woman--because a samurai is a larger than life individual, with no end of self-mastery. We don't allow ignorant words to control our actions.

1.3.1.7.2 Martial arts

"You must study fully other martial arts and not deviate even a little from the Way of the warrior."

Samurai and the martial arts go together. All samurai practiced martial arts, in the old days. For Miyamoto, certainly, his main abiding interest in life was martial arts and the above quote demonstrates his belief that you should be familiar with as many martial arts as possible. For the aspiring 21st century samurai, as well, it is recommended that you know at least one form of physical self-defence. Although a modern samurai may be found in more places than the battlefield, these days, our entire philosophy is predicated on the assumption that we can defend ourselves and the ones we love, in true warrior fashion. As a result, we need at least have a basic ability to defend ourselves. Being helpless is not compatible with the samurai life; not even for the modern samurai, whose battlefield may be no more threatening than an office, a soccer field or a construction site. But what, exactly, was their philosophy on the martial arts? What secrets did Miyamoto, that swordsman without equal, leave behind to aid the aspiring modern samurai on their path to martial arts perfection? Although his advice had mainly to do with sword-fighting, there are three core instructions given by Miyamoto, which could be applied to success in any martial art. These can be divided into 1. Spirit, 2. Gaze and 3. Discipline.

Instruction Manual for the 21st Century Samurai

1.3.1.7 Conflict

1. Spirit.

"In strategy your spiritual bearing must not be any different from normal."

First and foremost, in any martial art, you must have the correct mental attitude. That correct attitude, according to Miyamoto, was to polish what he called the "twofold spirit (of) heart and mind." The spirit of the mind refers to developing wisdom; we should "learn public justice, distinguish between good and evil, study the Ways of different arts one by one." In other words, Miyamoto believed you should learn about as many different arts and areas of knowledge as you possibly can. Miyamoto believed every discipline had something to teach us about martial matters, and so he recommended studying anything at all related to martial arts or the warrior life. This included not only fully studying all martial arts, but also any other discipline at all related to the warrior or the martial artist's life. The point being, any time away from actual combat should be spent in study that will aid our future combat. This knowledge, honed and ready, would be at our disposal at that split second when we need to make a decision. This ethic of immediacy and quick decisions were a general samurai rule, but even more so in the areas of martial arts and combat, where a moment's hesitation or an uninformed decision could mean death.

The spirit of the heart, on the other hand, referred to developing a kind of "attitude" towards life. As Miyamoto put it, "Both in fighting and in everyday life you should be determined though calm. Meet the situation without tenseness yet not recklessly, your spirit settled yet unbiased. Even when your spirit is calm do not let your body relax, and when your body is relaxed do not let your spirit slacken. Do not let your spirit be influenced by your body, or your body be influenced by your spirit. Be neither insufficiently spirited nor over spirited. An elevated spirit is weak and a low spirit is weak. Do not let the enemy see your spirit."

1.3.1.7 Conflict

This sums up Miyamoto's instruction on the all-important "twofold spirit of heart and mind"; the spirit of the warrior. Miyamoto believed that capturing this spirit was the first requirement for success in any martial art. Not only that, Miyamoto considered it essential for a warrior to "maintain the combat stance in everyday life and to make your everyday stance your combat stance." This referred to both combat stance and the twofold spirit of heart and mind. This way, a samurai should always be battle ready and would continuously hone their skill and familiarity with the twofold spirit of the warrior.

2. Gaze.

"The gaze should be large and broad. This is the twofold gaze 'Perception and Sight'."

Of paramount importance to Miyamoto's martial arts success was something most fighters neglect--the proper gaze. He advocated developing your peripheral vision, so that you could observe and notice anything, without the need to turn your head, move your eyes or in any other way indicate to the enemy what you are thinking. As Miyamoto put it: "It is necessary in strategy to be able to look to both sides without moving the eyeballs." This, like the twofold spirit of heart and mind, should be employed and developed at all times, not only in a combat situation. This way, the samurai is always prepared and, what is more, will more quickly develop proficiency in this "twofold gaze of perception and sight."

3. Discipline.

"Any man who wants to master the essence of my strategy must research diligently, training morning and evening. Thus can he polish his skill, become free from self, and realize extraordinary ability."

Instruction Manual for the 21st Century Samurai

1.3.1.7 Conflict

Simply put, Miyamoto believed it was necessary to devote a consistent and diligent effort towards the martial arts. This may seem like a simple point, but by modern standards, this "work ethic" is something to be found only in Olympic athletes and world class professionals. We, however, must be similarly "world class." It is a samurai's obligation to be so, in general, but especially in the area of the martial arts, which is the samurai's main area of speciality. One of the more significant points on Miyamoto's personal "strategy code" was "the Way is in the training." And this simple directive is far more profound than it may seem. If a samurai could diligently practice their martial art and practice the twofold way of the mind, spirit and gaze, their martial arts progress, according to Miyamoto, would be assured.

This appears to be a simple secret but, like all of Miyamoto's wisdom, it is sometimes the simplest and most elegant solutions that are the most profound and the most difficult to achieve, in practice. Given Miyamoto's record and his legendary status, I think we can be confident Miyamoto's "samurai solutions" to training in the martial arts are as close to the authoritative manual as we could possibly hope for.

1.3.1.7.3 Strategy

"Strategy is the craft of the warrior."

Whether you are facing another samurai, with a katana blade, or sparring with an aggressive colleague in a workplace setting, the famous ronin, Miyamoto, believed strategy was the most essential element of defeating an enemy. Mere force of arms was not enough. Martial arts prowess is a fine thing, but if we are ever pitted against an enemy who understands strategy, we will lose, no matter how strong we are. So we must be the one who understands strategy, if we are to emerge the victor in a conflict situation. As Miyamoto put

Instruction Manual for the 21st Century Samurai

1.3.1.7 Conflict

it: "one man can beat ten men, so a thousand men can beat ten thousand." The one element that made this possible was proper strategy.

So, what was Miyamoto's strategy? What were the winning methods that made him the legendary duelist that he was? We are speaking, here, of simple combat strategies, but Miyamoto had a profound and spiritual philosophy on life, which he called "strategy". This philosophy expounded the virtues of learning about all arts and professions and applying their wisdom to combat and the warrior life. More can be read about this philosophy in the chapter titled "Prowess"(1.3.1.2.3). This philosophy can help us defeat our enemies, but for the purposes of this chapter, we will stick to Miyamoto's numerous duel-specific fighting strategies. The ronin master had a multitude of duelling strategies, which he gave an assortment of poetic names, such as "holding down a pillow". The following twelve strategies form what we believe to be the most fundamental "samurai solutions" offered by the master, to help us prevail over any enemy that life may throw at us.

1.3.1.7.3.1 "Depending on the place."

Using location to your advantage, you can improve your odds against any enemy. For example, Miyamoto recommended pushing your enemy into an inconvenient location--such as a place with awkward footing, a place with sun in their eyes, or a place that was generally alarming to your enemy. What is more, you should dog the enemy's steps, never leaving them alone. The master stressed the importance of "not letting him see his situation." This way they will have a general feeling of uncertainty and may, in fact, trip over something. This could work in hand to hand combat, but also, metaphorically, when sparring with any sort of enemy. Maneuver them into an uncomfortable place and strike before they are even able to determine where they are.

Instruction Manual for the 21st Century Samurai

1.3.1.7 Conflict

1.3.1.7.3.2 "To know the times."

Timing was an important concept for Miyamoto. He said "there is timing in everything" and considered it essential for a warrior to get a sense for timing. By this strategy, he taught us that duels were won "Attack in an unsuspected manner, knowing his metre and modulation and the appropriate timing." And so, this strategy is composed of simply learning to observe your enemy's timing. That alone can win battles. Whether an actual battle or a battle of wits, a sudden deviation from expected timing can help win the day.

1.3.1.7.3.3 "Holding down a pillow."

If someone is victimizing you--at work, or in any situation--get the upper hand and keep it. Much like holding a pillow over someone's head, you should never let the enemy lift their head; you should never let the enemy gain control of the situation. As Miyamoto put it: "it is bad to be led about by the enemy. You must always be able to lead the enemy about." Lead your enemy into a situation and lead them into another situation before they can react. Keep their head down at all times and you will be the decider in this conflict. It is true a samurai avoids conflict, but when once an enemy has stepped on the tiger's tail, you should unleash the full fury of your warrior skills to cut down the enemy. Remember Miyamoto's words: "When you sacrifice your life, you must make fullest use of your weaponry. It is false not to do so, and to die with a weapon yet undrawn."

1.3.1.7.3.4 "Crossing at a ford."

A ship's captain crosses a body of water at its narrowest point. In a conflict, we assess the situation and identify the weakest point in

Instruction Manual for the 21st Century Samurai

1.3.1.7 Conflict

our enemy's defenses. Just like a ship's captain, we cross the water by the easiest route, to get to our destination. As Miyamoto puts it: "To cross at a ford means to attack the enemy's weak point, and to put yourself in an advantageous position."

1.3.1.7.3.5 "To know collapse."

If an enemy "loses his timing" and loses the rhythm of their movement, they will "collapse"--meaning they will be thrown off balance. According to this strategy "you must utterly cut the enemy down so that he does not recover his position." You cannot let the opportunity of your enemy's collapse to slip through your fingers. If you let it pass "he may recover and not be so negligent thereafter."

1.3.1.7.3.6 "To become the enemy."

Miyamoto said "you must put yourself in the enemy's position. If you think, 'Here is a master of the Way, who knows the principles of strategy', then you will surely lose." It is conventional wisdom that, in a fight, you shouldn't think about what the other guy is going to do to you, but rather, what you are going to do to the other guy. Miyamoto, amazingly, said the same thing, hundreds of years ago. You should not see your enemy as strong; but rather, you should concentrate only on how completely your chosen strategy will defeat them. Becoming the enemy, you can see they are not indestructible; you can learn to see their fears and vulnerabilities. By empathizing with your enemy, you can also develop a knack for guessing their intentions and so you can more easily react with the right strategy.

Instruction Manual for the 21st Century Samurai

1.3.1.7 Conflict

1.3.1.7.3.7 "To release four hands."

Four hands refers to two enemies locked in mortal combat and tied in a stalemate. If this situation occurs, this strategy tells us to "abandon this spirit and win through an alternative resource." Upon realizing we are locked in a stalemate, we should instantly abandon our strategy and quickly employ a new strategy. The point here is to retain the upper hand and turn a stalemate into a surprise attack.

1.3.1.7.3.8 "To move the shade."

Is your enemy hiding their hand? Are you unsure what kind of weaponry they have? According to this strategy, "when you cannot see the enemy's position, indicate that you are about to attack strongly, to discover his resources" and then it is possible to fight the enemy, as usual. It is basically a false attack; what the boxing world calls a "feint". By pretending to attack, we can size up the enemy. Even if we are not dealing with swordplay, but with a conflict in our workplace or any other life situation, we can still be confident that our enemy will pull out their biggest guns, if they are expecting a big attack. Their weaponry no longer secret, you can now strategize and plan a way to disarm them in a real fight.

1.3.1.7.3.9 "To pass on."

When squaring off against an enemy, you can influence their attitude. The enemy will likely be sizing you up, as much as you are sizing them up. By observing you so closely, they cannot help but mimic you, to some degree. If you exhibit a certain timing, or rhythm, they will follow your rhythm. You can then use that created rhythm to throw your enemy off guard, by suddenly striking with an unexpected rhythm. Or you can influence the enemy by "relaxing your body and spirit and then, catching on to the moment the enemy relaxes, attack strongly and quickly," Miyamoto referred to this method as "getting someone drunk" with the feeling of languor or casual relaxation, which can be taken advantage of.

Instruction Manual for the 21st Century Samurai

1.3.1.7 Conflict

1.3.1.7.3.10 "To cause loss of balance."

The element of surprise. This is conventional wisdom, but that doesn't make it any less important to overall success in combat. According to Miyamoto, "Many things can cause a loss of balance. One cause is danger, another is hardship, and another is surprise." It is useful to surprise the enemy, but it is equally valuable to force your enemy into a dangerous or difficult situation and so put them off balance. Once you have succeeded in doing this, "without allowing him space for breath to recover from the fluctuation of spirit, you must grasp the opportunity to win."

1.3.1.7.3.11 "To crush."

This simple strategy is, much like all simple strategies, deceptively important. When engaged in conflict, you must attack the enemy completely, "regarding him as being weak." You should not use half measures. Much like the saying "when fighting for your life you must make full use of your weaponry" we must not neglect an ounce of strength when we strike. It should be a confident, full-forced blow--always. Or, as Miyamoto put it, "It is essential to crush him all at once. The primary thing is not to let him recover his position even a little." If a samurai is forced to fight, they are as unstoppable as an approaching train. It should never be otherwise, even for a moment, until the enemy is at your feet.

1.3.1.7.3.12 "To penetrate the depths."

This is the ultimate in warrior intimidation tactics. But, in true samurai form, we don't intimidate by crude threats or beating our chest like an ape--no, we do so by subtle, masterly tactics. As Miyamoto puts it: "with this principle of 'penetrating the depths' we can destroy the enemy's spirit in its depths, demoralising him by quickly changing our spirit." In other words, along with defeating

1.3.1.7 Conflict

the enemy superficially, by deflecting their sword, we also seek to defeat them "in their depths" by disquieting them. This is similar to throwing them off balance, or surprising them. But even more so, this is an even deeper tactic of making the enemy feel defeated, inside, before we have dealt our killing blow. As Miyamoto puts it, we do this by "changing our spirit". Alternating between extremely different attitudes, speeds and timings, we can make the enemy so uncertain, they lose their fighting spirit.

Instruction Manual for the 21st Century Samurai

1.3.1.8 Family

"To be filial to my parents."

One of the points of Yamamoto's personal "Nabeshima code", the above quote applies, in fact, not only to parents but to a samurai's entire family and clan. The idea of "filial piety" or loyalty to one's family is a very Confucian idea--originating from the great Chinese philosopher, Confucius. But, as outlined in the chapter of this book titled "Spirituality"(1.3.1.6), although they were primarily Zen Buddhists, the samurai spiritual recipe was composed of many ingredients, including one or two Confucian ideas.

This ideal of filial piety was very compatible with the overall samurai ethics of service, loyalty and responsibility. Concerning the family, therefore, samurai strove to be what would nowadays be called "the perfect son", "the perfect father" or the perfect anything which a samurai may wind up becoming. So, how exactly did the samurai try to arrange their family lives? What ideals guided them?

As usual, when dealing with any matter outside of actual battle, Yamamoto, the palace samurai, had more to say than Miyamoto, the ronin of the road. Some may be scared by the prospect of trying to become the "perfect" anything, as far as family goes. But, it is important to remember our general mission as a samurai is self-mastery. Quests for perfection are our passion, not our fear, so we must learn to abandon old habits, which cause us to repel from seeking perfection. In typical samurai fashion, we will seek for self-mastery and yet accept the flaws of others. As part and parcel to our self-development, we must take the role of the strong one and help and accept those who are floundering or more in need of support or assistance. When we can come to fully understand that this is our role, as a samurai, we will lose all fear, strive to be the "perfect" everything and so begin on the true warrior path. The areas of a samurai's family life are best divided into 1. Family duty, 2. Discord and 3. Clan.

Instruction Manual for the 21st Century Samurai

1.3.1.8.1 Family duty

"From the time he is young, the child should liken his parents to the master."

Modern sons and daughters are inculcated with the billion dollar youth culture industry, which generally does nothing to encourage communication between generations. This culture is mainly created by the business world, for marketing purposes, and has little or nothing to do with encouraging family togetherness or anything approaching ethics. As a result of irresponsible creation of bad teen movies and other destructive influences, it has become commonplace for youth to disrespect their parents.

But things were not at all like this during samurai days. Quite the opposite, it was a samurai son or daughter's duty to respect and serve their parents and the rest of their family--at least to some degree, as a samurai would their master. Yamamoto's quote makes this crystal clear. Not only did he mention it in Hagakure, he went so far as to take it as a substantial point in his personal code of conduct. That illustrates how important this concept was to him, and, likely, to samurai in general.

Before you turn away from the samurai path, imagining a situation of servitude and parental exploitation, consider the following important point: we are talking about a samurai parent, not the stereotypical tyrannical and out of touch parent we know from all the farcical teen movies. To treat a samurai parent like a master is to have a symbiotic servant/servant relationship because--being samurai both--you are both advanced in the ways of selfless service. In that type of situation, there is no room for exploitation. Not only is it unlikely, if parent and child follow the samurai path outlined in this book, it is not even a possibility that exploitation could occur. On the contrary, for a child, the full and attentive service of a parent who is a high example of strength and worldly competence is

1.3.1.8 Family

something close to a satisfaction of everything a child needs, to confidently walk up that steep hill to adulthood.

Children need and want a strong, yet nurturing, helping hand and there is no one better than the samurai to provide that. So what is the samurai solution to family duty? Filial piety. The Confucian ideal of loyalty sums up the samurai view of family. For more on the type of samurai parent we would hope to make "master", in this way, see the chapter titled "Setting an example"(1.3.1.4.2). Of course, not everyone is blessed with samurai training and family breakdowns are common enough these days. By the time you pick up this book, your family relations may have already reached the point of no return. If this is so, and your parent/child relations are closer to something you'd see in a bad teen movie, then see the chapter titled "Discord"(1.3.1.8.2). You may be happy to know there are cases where it is acceptable to walk away from a situation which damages your samurai dignity and self-respect. A samurai is all about resilience and selfless service, but they should never permit themselves to be treated like a door-mat.

1.3.1.8.2 Discord

"A person of little merit is not at peace but walks about making trouble and is in conflict with all."

It is the duty of the samurai, in family relations--as in a work situation--to minimize conflict or bad feeling. Much like in the workplace, teamwork among your own is an essential part of the samurai ethic and everything possible should be done to promote it. But, there is a difference between being dutiful and being a door-mat. It may be our duty to offer selfless service, but the master/servant relationship has a unique character, in samurai terms. A samurai chooses to serve a master and does so out of respect and love, not because they are being forced. Service to them is not demeaning; service is an expression of their prowess and their pride; they serve because only they are strong enough to serve with

1.3.1.8 Family

such flawless perfection and such consummate ability. It is a source of pride to them. Given this, you can imagine that samurai were the perfect retainer; the perfect lieutenant to serve the greatest and most noble lord in the land and single-handedly bring about the most legendary of victories. The sheer quality of their service was such.

But this is a uniquely respectful and symbiotic master/servant relationship and it must not alter from this dignified state. If a lord abuses their servant, it is no longer a situation of service--it becomes the situation of a victim. A samurai has no place in the role of a victim and should never allow themself to assume that kind of position. If such a situation develops, it is acceptable--even for the service-focused samurai--to walk away, because there is no longer a master. A samurai needs a master, even if they are a ronin. Their master could be their family, their lover, their ideals--but they are there to serve, not to cringe under someone's cruel fist. If you want to be a samurai's master, you must behave like one.

So what is the samurai solution to dealing with a dysfunctional family relationship? Keep in mind Yamamoto's words: "It is because a samurai has correct manners, that he is admired." This is the ideal around which you should fashion your family relations. But, of course, even a samurai can reach the end of their rope. If a family relation resists all your formidable attempts to make it harmonious, it is not acceptable to allow yourself to be debased. You can walk away--for a while or for good--but apart from that extreme circumstance, keep in mind this should only be a last resort. We should direct all our formidable, well-developed powers to try to keep family together. Remember, it is, ultimately, the samurai ethic to serve our family and treat our samurai parents as we would the noblest lord. This is not only a samurai ethic, but a very significant one. This is not easy, sometimes. It's a whole lot easier to simply disrespect your parents and blame them for everything wrong in your life, as all the bad teen movies tell us we should. But such a low and easy road is not the samurai way. Taking the higher, more challenging path is what we thrive on.

1.3.1.8.3 Clan

"An ancestor's good or evil can be determined by the conduct of his descendants."

Japan's indigenous Shinto religion was one of animism; it was nature and ancestor worship, with a significant amount of complex rites and magical mysteries. The samurai, being Japanese to the core, could not be complete without at least some Shinto influence. Some went so far as to offer their invaluable service to a local Shinto deity, in exchange for protection or guidance. But it is likely all samurai took the idea of ancestor worship seriously.

As the above quote demonstrates, Yamamoto believed in an idea common to those who practiced ancestor worship--namely, that how we conduct ourselves during this life directly reflects on our parents and everyone who came before them. Even if seen with a cold and scientific eye, this perspective had a profound and often positive psychological effect. If you are acting independently and your actions reflect on no one but yourself, you will be a lot less responsible in your choices--you won't care quite as much as you would if your entire blood line is being affected by every choice you make in this world.

What is more, if a parent committed a serious crime or incurred a great dishonor, a child had the option to "redeem their line" by acting in a way that is above reproach. In this way, they will resist the urge to emulate their parent's faults and will instead keep their minds on their lofty ancestors. Families often celebrated these ancestors as something close to deities, and so the ancestor-worshipping child had more than one parental role model. If their parent's model did not meet their needs, they had a host of lofty and celebrated ancestor, with passed down tales of their accomplishments, to serve as their role models.

So what is the samurai solution to family honor? Yamamoto considered it essential to remember your ancestors in everything you do and to strive to do your progenitors proud. This is a big

1.3.1.8 Family

perspective shift for the modern person, who often considers their ancestors--or even their parents--irrelevant to their lives. This ancestor worship also helps us to have patience with, and to willingly serve, our own parents. Because to abandon or disregard them is much less likely if you have an entire legion of ghostly ancestors to consider, outside of the small world of you and your parents. "Honor" here should be understood in strictly samurai terms.

When speaking of an overly critical samurai's boorish behavior, Yamamoto said: "It is because a samurai has correct manners, that he is admired. Speaking of other people in this way is no different from an exchange between low class spearmen. It is vulgar." Yamamoto stressed that a samurai should be worldly enough to know the world is "full of unseemly situations" and that not everything will measure up to samurai ideals. A samurai should be worldly enough to recognize and accept that--his or her concern is mainly their own ethics, not that of others. It is the samurai's duty to be the strong one, not to use strong arm tactics to force our will on others. Bullying is unseemly and beneath samurai dignity. Preserving family honor, therefore, does not mean imposing our ethics on others. On the contrary, a samurai is tough with themselves, easy on others and makes compassion their compass. Preserving family honor, from a samurai perspective, has nothing to do with trying to control and dominate others. It is 100% about setting a good example, by our own impeccable samurai standards.

1.3.1.9 Arts and Education

"The warrior's is the twofold Way of pen and sword."

Back in the misty ages of feudal Japan, you could identify a samurai by the two swords they wore at their waist. These warriors could also be identified, no doubt, by the scrolls of poetry hanging from their belts. Haiku, painting and calligraphy were established past-times of the warrior class. It was not at all unusual or unacceptable for a tough-as-nails fighter, with a sword or a spear at their back, to be seen sitting down to write verse about the beauty of the morning dew. This was a genteel class of warrior. Although it was documented that women were not excluded from being samurai, and especially excelled in horseback archery, samurai might still be appropriately described as "gentlemen warriors."

As stated in the chapter titled "The Three Masters"(1.2), the palace samurai, Yamamoto, differed in opinion from Miyamoto, the ronin, concerning the arts. Miyamoto famously said that you should "become acquainted with every art" as part of your samurai code and to aid in developing over-all understanding of his concept of "strategy". But Yamamoto said, "the person who practices an art is an artist, not a samurai, and one should have the intention of being called a samurai." He accepted the practice of calligraphy or some similar "samurai art" as a past-time, if there were no battle to fight, but he generally implied that a warrior should stick to martial matters and not dabble in other areas. But, in spite of himself, Yamamoto seems to still hold some of Miyamoto's beliefs, concerning art's relevancy to the warrior's life, when he said: "The proper manner of calligraphy is nothing other than not being careless, but in this way one's writing will simply be sluggish and stiff . One should go beyond this and depart from the norm. This principle applies to all things." By saying this, Yamamoto showed that he in fact agreed with Miyamoto--that art has something to

1.3.1.9 Arts and Education

teach the samurai and vice versa. The tips given by the masters, concerning how a samurai approaches the arts and scholarship can be summarized in the following three creative areas: 1. The pen, 2. The sword and 3. The art of living.

1.3.1.9.1 The pen

"Become acquainted with every art."

Miyamoto was known to paint, write poetry, practice carpentry, farm the land and generally tried to learn as many arts and trades as possible. He could be called a jack of all trades. But as for being a "master of none", Miyamoto was far from that! He was the greatest swordsman of his age and developed a quick knack for almost everything he tried. He credits this easy skill with his idea of "strategy", which could be summed up in the practice of "intuitive judgment". This profound life philosophy stated, basically, that all arts and trades had things in common and the more you learned, the more you gained an intuitive understanding of what it means to be skillful, in general. For a more detailed explanation of this complex philosophy, see the chapter titled "Prowess"(1.3.1.2.3).

Yamamoto, as well, did not entirely disapprove of arts as recreation. Especially calligraphy, painting and poetry were smiled upon, being dignified arts--appropriate for a cultured warrior. When Yamamoto spoke of how calligraphy should involve more than just competence, he was expressing a very profound underpinning of the samurai ethic: you should not only seek to be competent to the bare minimum, you should take the difficult road and seek perfection. Given this, you can see why Yamamoto did not consider calligraphy to be in conflict with his warrior ways--to have a bunch of adeptly executed scrolls of calligraphy hanging from your walls demonstrated to anyone who walked into your chambers that you understood the samurai ethic of striving for perfection. This ethic and this sort of warrior's "perfection practice" could be applied to any art, not only to arts of the brush.

Instruction Manual for the 21st Century Samurai

1.3.1.9 Arts and Education

But, it should be noted Yamamoto put the arts as the very last item on the samurai "to do" list. He recommended study first. To Yamamoto, most of the samurai's responsibility to "the pen" came in the form of study and acquiring knowledge. He stated that a samurai should study often, "setting his mind to work without putting things off." His priority was to study the master; the clan; the local history and the ways and history of the warrior.

This was very in line with the samurai strategy of life. Both Miyamoto and Yamamoto believed in being decisive and making quick, confident decisions. In order to make fast choices, while still making wise choices, it was necessary to study everything about it beforehand. So, scholarly pursuits were not only considered appropriate, by the masters, it was the duty of every samurai to study and so ensure that we could be quick and decisive, the way a real samurai should be.

So, what is the samurai solution to arts and education? They are both essential. When not fighting, in fact, study and art are an obligation. Crude, ignorant warriors may've existed, in feudal Japan, but they could not properly be called samurai. This was an educated class--even if, as in the case of Miyamoto, their education came mostly from the road and the teachings of those they met along the way. Consider it your duty to practice perfection, through the arts, and to develop a quick and ready intuitive judgment, through study and tireless commitment to education. Anything less would make you a simple swordsman, a strong-arm, or something less than a full warrior--in the samurai sense.

1.3.1.9.2 The sword

"A warrior you must study fully other martial arts and not deviate even a little from the Way of the warrior."

What is a samurai without a sword? In the old days, martial arts were the single most important element of the samurai's life. It was,

Instruction Manual for the 21st Century Samurai

1.3.1.9 Arts and Education

basically, what their lives revolved around. Nowadays, battle and combat are the province of a chosen few and most of us will never have to employ martial skills of any kind, during our entire life. But that does not exclude us from living as the samurai did. As this book clearly demonstrates, their philosophies and outlooks are applicable to all aspects of life. But, given how central the martial arts were to the samurai, it is advisable for the aspiring 21st century samurai to practice a martial art, a serious sport or, at least, some activity that conditions and tempers the body.

It is an obligation, in a sense, to keep yourself in good shape. If you are taking the role of the strong one--the defender--then you cannot be defenseless. You need to be able to fend off an attack, if it comes. The safety of your master and the integrity of your service depend on it. Miyamoto, that unmatched duelist, suggested that you "maintain the combat stance in everyday life and to make your everyday stance your combat stance." In order to be able to do this, it is recommended you learn at least one combat stance, and one form of self-defence, even if it is nothing more than a few boxing classes. But, in truth, any sport that could keep you on your toes, ready to jump into action, is sufficient. Jogging, skateboarding, volleyball--anything that conditions your body to react with energy and precision will, at least, keep you from the state of being defenseless in an emergency. But, of course, a samurai strives to take the difficult path--leaving the path of ease for non-warriors--and so it is best to become proficient at self-defence. A black belt in judo is going to do more to assure adequate defense than competing in beach volleyball.

The sword was so essential to the samurai that is was referred to as the "soul of the samurai." Nowadays, of course, the sword has no real use. You might be tempted to think the soul of the samurai has therefore become obsolete, but that isn't so. That is because swordfighting is extremely useful as an art form. To learn Kendo, the Japanese art of sword fighting, not only helps us to assert our identity as 21st century samurai, it also gives us an opportunity to

Instruction Manual for the 21st Century Samurai

1.3.1.9 Arts and Education

practice the "art of perfection". As stated in the chapter titled "The pen"(1.3.1.9.1), the masters recommended studying calligraphy in order to learn how to perfectly execute an art form.

Given that samurai strive to take the most challenging of paths and not only succeed, but excel, an art can give them the perfect outlet to, so to speak, "practice perfection". There is probably no better way to practice perfection than with Kendo. Not only because it is very "samurai", but also because it simultaneously tempers and strengthens the body. In this way, it fulfills more than one of our obligations. Any martial art, sport or athletic pursuit can be used to "practice perfection" in this way, while simultaneously fulfilling our obligation to be in good shape.

1.3.1.9.3 The art of living

"Do nothing which is of no use."

On top of the arts of the pen and the sword, the samurai path itself was an art form. The religion of choice was Zen Buddhism, which has, at its center, the idea of zazen. Zazen is the practice of perpetual meditation. Unlike other Buddhist schools, who only do sitting meditation, zazen practitioners learn to meditate when they are sitting, standing, making tea, sweeping the floor--or during any time at all, from dawn to dusk. The monk, Dōgen, said "beyond doubt, you should recognize that this practice is the complete and whole Way of the Buddha Dharma: there is nothing to compare it to." In other words, Dōgen believed that anything less than constant zazen meditation could not possibly lead you to full enlightenment. Given this, it becomes clear that a true samurai--fully practicing zazen--did not only study art, but made a constant art out of the simple act of living. For more information on zazen, the most important and difficult of samurai pursuits, see the chapter titled "Enlightenment"(1.3.1.2.2).

1.3.1.9 Arts and Education

So what is the samurai solution to living life? Practice zazen. It is known that samurai recommended artistic pursuits as a method to "practice perfection." Creating the perfect calligraphy scroll, the perfect painting of a mountain or the perfect haiku all helped the samurai to become acquainted with methods to achieve perfection. This practice in perfection helped them to master themselves, hone their character and perfect their warrior skills. But of all the arts, there is none better than to master the art of living. In this way, Dōgen's zazen was ideally suited to the samurai.

Instruction Manual for the 21st Century Samurai

1.3.1.10 Leisure

"Whatever you do should be done for the sake of your master and parents, the people in general, and for posterity."

Even a samurai gets leisure time, now and again. So, when you find yourself reclined on your futon, sword propped against the wall, with no particular battle to fight--then what is a samurai to do? All three masters give a good deal of practical advice on how a samurai should craft and discipline themselves--more than enough to keep you busy and on your feet, even when there is no immediate battle at hand. So get up, grab your sword and head down that long and difficult path of samurai self-perfection. What, exactly, is that path? What are the samurai obliged to do with their free time?

Yamamoto sums it up nicely in the above quote. Samurai are all about selfless service and honor; whatever you do is for others or for posterity. That is the general message about how you should spend your free time. For more specific leisure time activities, we will divide the suggestions of the three masters into three areas: 1. Perspective, 2. Refinement and 3. Training, practice and more training. The arts are another valid leisure time pursuit. For advice on that topic, see the chapter titled "Arts and Education"(1.3.1.9).

1.3.1.10.1 Perspective

"Be determined, though calm."

There is always an opportunity to practice the proper samurai perspective in life. Just sitting and looking out the window is an opportunity to practice the right perspective. So, it is not necessary to be in the heat of battle, to train ourselves. The careful study of zazen and the teachings of the Buddhist masters is a useful way to spend your free time and also learn the perspective of the samurai.

Instruction Manual for the 21st Century Samurai

1.3.1.10 Leisure

As Zen was the religion of these enlightened warriors, most of the samurai perspective can be learned by coming to understand zazen. For more information on this, read the chapter titled "Enlightenment"(1.3.1.2.2).

In addition to zazen, however, there are more insights of the masters, concerning the proper perspective for the aspiring modern samurai. These gems of wisdom on samurai perspective can be summed up in the following five points:

1. "Exclude self-interest, and make an effort, and you will not go far from your mark."
In true samurai fashion, your duty is to abandon the petty fears that hold back most people and forge ahead with unflagging force. Like perfectly executed calligraphy--this is a simple, minimalist message with a wealth of significance. By following this simple formula, the samurai does great things.

2. "Setting one's heart right every morning and evening, one is able to live as though his body were already dead."
The samurai had no fear of death. As outlined in this book, the samurai had many ways of accomplishing this fearlessness. But a primary way was to abandon self-interest by training their mind to act as if they were already dead. Much like the conventional wisdom that we should live each day as if it were our last, the samurai believed in keeping this perspective honed--morning, noon and night.

3. "Learning is a good thing."
Education was a very serious responsibility for the samurai. Ignorance was for unskilled swordsmen and lackeys. A samurai was expected to be learned, and always seeking to expand that learning. Yamamoto also said that "it is not good to settle into a set of opinions... at first putting forth great effort to be sure that you have grasped the basics, then practicing so that they may come to fruition is something that will never stop for your whole lifetime.

1.3.1.10 Leisure

Do not rely on following the degree of understanding that you have discovered, but simply think, 'This is not enough.'" You should always say "this is not enough" and should consider study never-ending. The samurai was a perpetual student in life's university.

4. "If one were to say what it is to do good, in a single word it would be to endure suffering. Not enduring is bad without exception."
The samurai perspective was a Buddhist one, for the most part, and suffering is seen as an inescapable reality in Buddhist thought. A samurai, therefore, had a responsibility to endure suffering. It is the samurai's duty to be the strong one and so we cannot allow ourselves to be defeated--not by enemies and not by circumstances. As Yamamoto said, "a person who becomes fatigued when unhappy is useless." Just as in all things, we must learn how to defend ourselves from the effects of unhappiness. Study of Buddhist philosophy and zazen can go a long way in helping us to deal with life's suffering.

5. "Fit oneself inwardly with intelligence, humanity and courage."
With all the codes, formulas and advice to be followed in this book, it can seem a bit overwhelming. But Yamamoto summed up the core of the samurai perspective in concise, elegant language when he said that intelligence, humanity and courage are the primary things for us to remember. For the aspiring modern samurai to remember these simple points, they can keep themselves on the samurai path.

1.3.1.10.2 Refinement

"It is because a samurai has correct manners that he is admired."

We can practice good manners in any situation. Whether we're visiting friends, family; interacting with strangers; preparing our clothes or arranging our living space--there is a chance to practice that elegant etiquette that should be a hallmark of the samurai

1.3.1.10 Leisure

warrior. The master, Yamamoto, had a lot to share about the traditional code of etiquette, which the samurai followed. His decades of life in the polite and cultured atmosphere of the palace taught him the authentic codes of behavior we can now follow, to forge ourselves into authentic modern samurai. Yamamoto's valuable insights can be summed up in the following three points:

1. "Meet people cordially at all times and without distraction."
In dealing with people, the samurai ideal is to give full attention and to be perfectly respectful. Yamamoto said, "one should look his listener in the eye." In addition, he suggested that a samurai should keep their conversation relevant as part of basic good manners and should avoid criticizing others. As Yamamoto put it: "A fault-finder will come to be punished by others." Guests should be met cordially and one should behave as if they are reluctant for their guests to leave. The samurai should maintain high standards of civility at all times.

2. "Inside the skin of a dog, outside the hide of a tiger."
A samurai prides themself on their appearance. "Skin of a dog" refers to the spartan and simple needs of the samurai, inside; "Hide of tiger" refers to the fact the samurai considered it important to project a pleasing and positive image to the world. It is not a question of vanity, but rather, it is two things: an extension of good manners and a method by which the samurai can "practice perfection." It is recommended that a samurai practice all forms of art, in order to "practice perfection" and so make their warrior skills more perfect--by extension. The art form of the samurai's appearance is no exception. Yamamoto said: "After I took up the attitude of a retainer, I never sat sloppily whether at home or in some other place." This one directive expresses the great importance the samurai put on the dignity of their appearance.

3. "Men with contriving hearts are lacking in duty. Lacking in duty, they will have no self-respect."

Instruction Manual for the 21st Century Samurai

1.3.1.10 Leisure

Yamamoto considered it a question of self-respect to keep your surroundings clean and tidy. Not only is it a question self-respect and dignity, but the samurai reconciles themself with the notion that death could come at any moment, even when they are alone at home. It is a samurai's duty to look neat, in neat surroundings, as a respectful way of greeting death. This ethic could be summed up in the words: "Even if you are aware that you may be struck down today and are firmly resolved to an inevitable death, if you are slain with an unseemly appearance, you will show your lack of previous resolve, will be despised by your enemy, and will appear unclean. For this reason it is said that both old and young should take care of their appearance." This explains why the samurai considered their personal appearance so important. By extension, the home is to be kept neat, as well, out of courtesy to others and as preparation for the samurai's always-imminent death.

1.3.1.10.3 Training, practice and more training

"The Way is in the training."

Continual training and practice was the mantra of the samurai. On top of continual learning, you should spend all your time training and advancing your skills, ever more so, on a daily basis. Yamamoto said, "throughout your life advance daily, becoming more skillful than yesterday, more skillful than today. This is never-ending" and this is the most basic thing we need to remember, when considering how the samurai approached training. We must have a firm work ethic, worthy of a hardened and disciplined warrior. So, when you are reclining in your dojo, gazing out the window at the peach tree blossoms and wondering, "what is a samurai to do?" Pick up a sword and practice.

What is the samurai solution to our training? Simple. Training, practice and more training. If we think about this, there is, in fact, no free time for a samurai. Practice and training is their perpetual past-time and these things end only in death. What with zazen, the

1.3.1.10 Leisure

arts, the occasional battle and the never-ending requirement of practice, a samurai never need lament that they have nothing to do. A samurai is a busy person! A samurai is obliged to keep busy. In the words of the Miyamoto: "do nothing which is of no use." For more advice on the various forms of training we could embark on, see the chapters titled "The Sword"(1.3.1.9.2), "Self-mastery" (1.3.1.2.1) and "Prowess"(1.3.1.2.3).

Instruction Manual for the 21st Century Samurai

1.4 Reference

Find the category your problem falls into and pick that which most closely resembles your problem. Turn to the chapter or page number indicated to find the "samurai solution" to your problem! You can also choose a single-word reference in "quick reference"(1.5), to lead you to the most appropriate solution.

1. Career

How should a samurai approach their career? 1.3.1.1 (p.13)
I want to be a leader. 1.3.1.1.1 (p.14)
I have made a mistake. 1.3.1.1.2 (p.15)
I want to learn on the job. 1.3.1.1.2 (p.15)
How should I relate to my colleagues? 1.3.1.1.3 (p.16)
I have conflict with a co-worker. 1.3.1.7.3 (p.54)
My employer is mistreating me. 1.3.1.8.2 (p.63)
I want to excel at my job. 1.3.1.1.1 (p.14)
I just lost my job. 1.3.1.1.2 (p.15)
I am retiring from my career. 1.3.1.10 (p.73)

2. Dreams

I want to fulfill my dreams. 1.3.1.2 (p.18)
How do I follow authentic samurai codes? 1.3.1.2.1 (p.19)
How can I be an authentic samurai? 1.3.1.2.1 (p.19)
I want to become enlightened. 1.3.1.2.2 (p.21)
I want to find spiritual perfection. 1.3.1.2.2 (p.21)
I want to become the very best. 1.3.1.2.3 (p.23)
I want to be the best samurai in history. 1.3.1.2.3 (p.23)
I want to realize an ambition. 1.3.1.2 (p.18)
I want to find true love. 1.3.1.3 (p.26)

3. Love

Should I remain faithful to my lover? 1.3.1.3.1 (p.26)
I want to give my partner true love. 1.3.1.3.2 (p.28)
My partner has faults. 1.3.1.3.3.1 (p.29)
How can I best communicate with my partner? 1.3.1.3.3.2 (p.30)
My partner is abusing me. 1.3.1.3.1 (p.26)
Should a samurai lie? 1.3.1.3.3.3 (p.30)
Should I look good for my partner? 1.3.1.3.3.4 (p.30)
I am in love. 1.3.1.3 (p.26)

Instruction Manual for the 21st Century Samurai

1.4 Reference

I want to make the perfect relationship. 1.3.1.3.1 (p.26)
I broke up with my partner. 1.3.1.3.2 (p.28)
We're encountering some difficulties in our relationship. 1.3.1.3.1 (p.26)

4. Children

I want to bring up my kids right. 1.3.1.4 (p.32)
My kids need discipline. 1.3.1.4.1 (p.32)
How do I set an example for my children? 1.3.1.4.2 (p.34)
I want my kids to grow up to be the best they can be. 1.3.1.4.3 (p.35)
I don't want to spoil my kids. 1.3.1.4.3 (p.35)

5. Death

How does a samurai view death? 1.3.1.5 (p.38)
I want to know how to approach my own death. 1.3.1.5.1 (p.38)
Someone close to me is sick or dying. 1.3.1.5.2 (p.39)
How do I deal with change? 1.3.1.5.3 (p.40)
How do I deal with aging and the passage of time? 1.3.1.2.2 (p.21)

6. Spirituality

What is a samurai's religion? 1.3.1.6 (p.42)
How should I approach the gods? 1.3.1.6.1 (p.42)
How should I approach ghosts and the supernatural? 1.3.1.6.2 (p.44)
What is the samurai view of the universe? 1.3.1.6.3 (p.46)
I want to achieve enlightenment. 1.3.1.2.2 (p.21)

7. Conflict

I am in conflict with someone. 1.3.1.7 (p.49)
How should I deal with insults? 1.3.1.7.1 (p.49)
I want to walk away from a provoking person. 1.3.1.7.1 (p.49)
I want to study martial arts. 1.3.1.7.2 (p.51)
How should a samurai approach the martial arts? 1.3.1.7.2 (p.51)
I want to defeat an enemy. 1.3.1.7.3 (p.54)
When should I walk away from a challenge? 1.3.1.7.1 (p.49)
I want to be physically ready to defend myself. 1.3.1.7.2 (p.51)

Instruction Manual for the 21st Century Samurai

1.4 Reference

8. Family

What is the samurai view of family? 1.3.1.8 (p.61)
I am conflicting with a member of my family. 1.3.1.8.2 (p.63)
My family member is abusing me. 1.3.1.8.2 (p.63)
What about my "family honor?" 1.3.1.8.3 (p.65)
I want to know how to do right by my family. 1.3.1.8.1 (p.62)
How did the samurai worship their ancestors? 1.3.1.8.3 (p.65)
My child has a problem. 1.3.1.4.1 (p.32)

9. Arts and Education

What kind of education should I get? 1.3.1.9 (p.67)
What should I study? 1.3.1.9.1 (p.68)
I want to become an artist. 1.3.1.9.1 (p.68)
I want to excel as an athlete. 1.3.1.9.2 (p.69)
Should I stay in good shape? 1.3.1.9.2 (p.69)
How should I live my life? 1.3.1.9.3 (p.71)
How should I look at life? 1.3.1.9.3 (p.71)
What should a samurai study? .1.3.1.9 (p.67)
I want to excel at my sport. 1.3.1.9.2 (p.69)
I want to become a skilled martial artist. 1.3.1.7.2 (p.51)
How does a samurai approach the "art of living?" 1.3.1.9.3 (p.71)

10. Free time (and general pursuits)

I have a lot of time on my hands. 1.3.1.10 (p.73)
What was the samurai outlook? 1.3.1.10.1 (p.73)
How can I succeed? 1.3.1.10.1.1 (p.74)
I want to live every day like it is my last. 1.3.1.10.1.2 (p.74)
How should I approach my education? 1.3.1.10.1.3 (p.74)
I am suffering. 1.3.1.10.1.4 (p.75)
How should a samurai behave? 1.3.1.10.1.5 (p.75)
I want to have good samurai manners, at all times. 1.3.1.10.2 (p.75)
I am having guests over. 1.3.1.10.2.1 (p.76)
How well should I groom myself? 1.3.1.10.2.2 (p.76)
How should I arrange my personal space? 1.3.1.10.2.3 (p.76)
Should I be training myself? 1.3.1.10.3 (p.77)
I want to practice samurai disciplines. 1.3.1.10.3 (p.77)
What perspective should a samurai maintain at all times? 1.3.1.10.1 (p.73)

Instruction Manual for the 21st Century Samurai

1.5 Quick Reference

Aging 1.3.1.2.2 (p.21)
Ambition 1.3.1.2 (p.18)
Ancestors 1.3.1.8.3 (p.65)
Appearance 1.3.1.10.2.2 (p.76)
Areas of life 1.3.1 (p.12)
Arts 1.3.1.9 (p.67)
Athletics 1.3.1.9.2 (p.69)
Attention 1.3.1.3.3.2 (p.30)
Attentiveness 1.3.1.3.3.2 (p.30)
Battle 1.3.1.7.3 (p.54)
Being an example 1.3.1.4.2 (p.34)
Book of Five Rings 1.2.1 (p.6)
Bosses 1.3.1.1.3 (p.16)
Buddhism 1.3.1.2.2 (p.21)
Bushido Code 1.2.2.2 (p.9)
Career 1.3.11 (p.13)
Change 1.3.1.5.3 (p.40)
Children 1.3.1.4 (p.32)
Choices 1.3.1.1.1 (p.14)
Clan 1.3.1.8.3 (p.65)
Cleanliness 1.3.1.10.2.2 (p.76)
Clothing 1.3.1.10.2.2 (p.76)
Codes of the samurai 1.3.1.2.1 (p.19)
Colleagues 1.3.1.1.3 (p.16)
Combat strategy 1.3.1.7.3 (p.54)
Conflict 1.3.1.7 (p.49)
Corporal punishment 1.3.1.4.1 (p.32)
Cosmology 1.3.1.6.3 (p.46)
Co-workers 1.3.1.1.3 (p.16)
Criticism 1.3.1.3.3.1 (p.29)
Death 1.3.1.5 (p.38)
Decisions 1.3.1.1.1 (p.14)
Defeat 1.3.1.5.3 (p.40)
Defeating an enemy 1.3.1.7.3 (p.54)
Deities 1.3.1.6.1 (p.42)
Devotion 1.3.1.3.1 (p.26)

Discipline 1.3.1.2.1 (p.19)
Disciplining children 1.3.1.4.1 (p.32)
Dōgen 1.2.3 (p.10)
Dreams 1.3.1.2 (p.18)
Dress/appearance 1.3.1.10.2.2 (p.76)
Education 1.3.1.9 (p.67)
Egotism (p.15)
Employees 1.3.1.1.3 (p.16)
Enlightenment 1.3.1.2.2 (p.21)
Enemies 1.3.1.7.3.6 (p.57)
Etiquette 1.3.1.10.2 (p.75)
Example for children 1.3.1.4.2 (p.34)
Exploitation 1.3.1.8.2 (p.63)
Faithfulness 1.3.1.3.1 (p.26)
Fame 1.3.1.2 (p.18)
Family 1.3.1.8 (p.61)
Family honor 1.3.1.8.3 (p.65)
Family duty 1.3.1.8.1 (p.62)
Family conflict 1.3.1.8.2 (p.63)
Family life 1.3.1.8 (p.61)
Faults 1.3.1.3.3.1 (p.29)
Friends 1.3.1.10.2.1 (p.76)
Ghosts 1.3.1.6.2 (p.44)
Gods 1.3.1.6.1 (p.42)
Good manners 1.3.1.10.2 (p.75)
Guests 1.3.1.10.2.1 (p.76)
Guiding children 1.3.1.4.2 (p.34)
Hagakure 1.2.2 (p.8)
Home 1.3.1.10.2.3 (p.76)
Honesty 1.3.1.3.3.3 (p.30)
Honor 1.3.1.8.3 (p.65)
Hygiene 1.3.1.10.2.2 (p.76)
Ignorance 1.3.1.7.1 (p.49)
Illness 1.3.1.5 (p.38)
Impermanence 1.3.1.5.3 (p.40)
Insults 1.3.1.7.1 (p.49)
Job 1.3.1.1 (p.13)

Instruction Manual for the 21st Century Samurai

1.5 Quick Reference

Kami 1.3.1.6.1 (p.43)
Keeping in shape 1.3.1.9.2 (p.69)
Leadership 1.3.1.1.1 (p.14)
Learning 1.3.1.9.1 (p.68)
Learn on the job 1.3.1.1.2 (p.15)
Leisure time 1.3.1.10 (p.73)
Lies 1.3.1.3.3.3 (p.30)
Living in the now 1.3.1.10.1.2 (p.74)
Living life 1.3.1.9.3 (p.71)
Losing a job 1.3.1.1.2 (p.15)
Love 1.3.1.3 (p.26)
Loyalty 1.3.1.3.1 (p.26)
Manners 1.3.1.10.2 (p.75)
Martial arts 1.3.1.7.2 (p.51)
Meditation 1.3.1.2.2 (p.21)
Mistakes 1.3.1.1.2 (p.15)
Miyamoto 1.2.1 (p.6)
Monk 1.2.3 (p.10)
Mysteries 1.3.1.6.2 (p.44)
Nabeshima Code(Yamamoto) 1.2.2.2 (p.8)
Nurturing 1.3.1.4.3 (p.35)
Perfection 1.3.1.9.3 (p.71)
Personal space 1.3.1.10.2.3 (p.76)
Politeness 1.3.1.10.2 (p.75)
Power 1.3.1.2.3 (p.23)
Practice 1.3.1.10.3 (p.77)
Provocation 1.3.1.7.1 (p.49)
Prowess 1.3.1.2.3 (p.23)
Poverty 1.3.1.2 (p.18)
Raising children 1.3.1.4 (p.32)
Relationships 1.3.1.3 (p.26)
Religion 1.3.1.6 (p.42)
Respect 1.3.1.3.3 (p.29)
Riches 1.3.1.2 (p.18)
Romance 1.3.1.3 (p.26)
Ronin 1.2.1 (p.6)
Rudeness(from us) 1.3.1.1.3 (p.16)

Rudeness(to us) 1.3.1.7.1 (p.49)
Samurai basics 1.3.1.10.1.5 (p.75)
Samurai code 1.3.1.2.1 (p.19)
Samurai cosmology 1.3.1.6.3 (p.46)
Samurai religion 1.3.1.6 (p.42)
Samurai Website (p.12)
Self-mastery 1.3.1.2.1 (p.19)
Setting example 1.3.1.4.2 (p.34)
Shinto 1.3.1.6.1 (p.43)
Shobogenzo (p.10)
Sickness 1.3.1.5 (p.38)
Skill 1.3.1.2.3 (p.23)
Socializing 1.3.1.10.2.1 (p.76)
Spartanism 1.3.1.2 (p.18)
Spirituality 1.3.1.6 (p.44)
Spoiled child 1.3.1.4.3 (p.35)
Starting a family 1.3.1.4 (p.32)
Strategy 1.3.1.7.3 (p.54)
Strategy Code(Miyamoto) 1.2.1.2 (p.6)
Success 1.3.1.10.1.1 (p.74)
Suffering 1.3.1.10.1.4 (p.75)
Supernatural 1.3.1.6.2 (p.44)
Surroundings 1.3.1.10.2.3 (p.76)
Taking the high road 1.3.1.7.1 (p.49)
The universe 1.3.1.6.3 (p.46)
Training 1.3.1.10.3 (p.77)
Universe 1.3.1.6.3 (p.46)
Victory 1.3.1.7.3 (p.54)
Violence 1.3.1.7 (p.49)
Vows 1.3.1.2.1 (p.19)
Wealth 1.3.1.2 (p.18)
Website (p.12)
Win a conflict 1.3.1.7.3 (p.54)
Worship 1.3.1.6.1 (p.42)
Yamamoto 1.2.2 (p.8)
Zazen 1.3.1.2.2 (p.21)
Zen Buddhism 1.3.1.2.2 (p.21)

1.6 Bibliography

William Scott Wilson, *Hagakure, The Book of the Samurai* (USA: Kondasha, 1992).

Victor Harris, *A Book of Five Rings* (New York: The Overlook Press, 1974).

Norman Waddell and Masao Abe, *The Heart of Dōgen's Shōbōgenzō* (New York: State University of New York Press, 2002).

Hubert Nearman, *Shōbōgenzō, The Treasure House of the Eye of the True Teaching* (Mount Shasta, CA: Shasta Abbey Press, 2007).

Kenji Tokitsu, *Miyamoto Musashi, His Life and Writings* (Boston, USA: Shambhala, 2004).

Made in the USA
Las Vegas, NV
19 December 2023

83077238R00049